One of the great needs of the hour centers on getting God's Word communicated relevantly and with authenticity. The lack of biblical understanding is desperate today—even in the church. Preachers must "preach the Word," but it must be done in a communicative, living, pertinent manner and with the power of the Holy Spirit. *Preaching with Relevance* addresses those issues in a most practical step-by-step, inspirational, and informative way. If every preacher would follow the patterns and practices outlined in this most helpful volume, the level of preaching would rise to a new effectiveness. I most heartily recommend this book to every God-called preacher of the Word.

—Lewis A. Drummond
Billy Graham Professor of Evangelism & Church Growth
Beeson Divinity School
Author of *Spurgeon: Prince of Preachers*

When love for God's Word and God's people become the priorities of the preacher, relevant expository preaching becomes a natural desire. Keith Willhite gives wise and experienced advice on fulfilling that desire with faithfulness to God and his people.

—Bryan Chapell
President, Covenant Theological Seminary
Author of *Christ-Centered Preaching*

Keith Willhite demonstrates that preaching can be biblically sound, rooted firmly in Scripture, and at the same time strikingly relevant to the lives of people. Through his ten strategies for expository preachers, he helps us understand how to accomplish both objectives more effectively.

—Michael Duduit
Editor, *Preaching* magazine

This book is an excellent refresher course for anyone who wants to preach with power, conviction, and relevance. Keith Willhite has provided a practical guide to preparing biblical sermons that connect with 21st-century audiences. The book is wonderfully practical. Though backed by an excellent understanding of critical communication theory, there's no stodgy stuff to wade through. Get it, read it, and put it into practice! Your preaching will never be the same.

—Dr. Ray Pritchard
Senior Pastor
Calvary Memorial Church, Oak Park, IL

PREACHING
WITH
Without
Dumbing Down
RELEVANCE

PREACHING WITH RELEVANCE

Without Dumbing Down

Keith Willhite

kregel
PUBLICATIONS

Grand Rapids, MI 49501

ISBN 0-8254-4114-5

Printed in the United States of America

1 2 3 4 5 / 05 04 03 02 01

To
Andy and Margie Anderson,
who first taught me to love relevant biblical preaching;

and to my sister, Shirley,
who introduced me to our Savior, Jesus, whom we preach!
2 Corinthians 4:5

Contents

Foreword   11

Acknowledgments   13

Introduction   15

1. Look from the Pew's Perspective   21

2. Get into a Good Argument   35

3. Whet an Appetite for God's Word   43

4. Use Applicational Wording   61

5. Bundle a Packaged Deal   73

6. Unite People, Purpose, and Proposition   81

7. Adjust the Questions   87

8. Tell 'n Show   95

9. Illustrate According to Purpose   103

10. Be Clear!   121

    Afterword   131

    Notes   135

Foreword

My Aunt Ginny was one of the great cooks of the twentieth century. That wasn't solely my verdict. All the members of our extended family shared that opinion. On Thanksgiving or Christmas we would all assemble at Aunt Ginny's house to enjoy a world-class dinner, arguably the finest feast served in New York City that day. The turkey, the stuffing, the potatoes, and the gravy were all superb, but the crowning moment of the meal came when Aunt Ginny served her desserts. If there is a Platonic ideal of mince or pumpkin pie, Aunt Ginny's came as close to it as any chef on earth.

You cannot imagine how stunned I was, therefore, to learn that my Aunt Ginny used cookbooks. In fact, she confessed that she got her piecrust recipe from Betty Crocker. And, furthermore, she didn't seem repentant! I thought that no world-class cook would ever take advice from someone else. Why would she follow a formula concocted by Mrs. Crocker when she could follow her own instincts for making desserts? But my Aunt Ginny was a modest woman. She knew she didn't know everything there was to know about cooking, and other devotees of the stove and oven could help her to excel.

Ministers can learn a lot from my Aunt Ginny. No matter how long we've been crafting sermons, none of us has achieved perfection. (After delivering some sermons that fell like wounded ducks before they reached the first row of pews, I've often wondered if I know anything at all about preaching!) All of us can still learn from others. A preacher or a teacher would do well to read at least one book on preaching every year. To coin a commercial phrase, we need to think about preaching again for the first time.

If you're just starting out in your calling, there are more appropriate texts to help you with preaching. But if you've been preaching awhile, then *Preaching with Relevance* might be the book for you to read this year. This book is practical, usable, and easy to understand. What is more, it does what it promises: It gives you strategies for preparing and communicating relevant biblical sermons. It mixes the ingredients from the recipe in proper proportions. I recommend it to you. And so would my Aunt Ginny.

—HADDON W. ROBINSON

Acknowledgments

Like most books, this one is the work of several people. I'm grateful in particular to Dr. Mark Bailey, Provost and Vice President of Academic Affairs at Dallas Theological Seminary, for adjusting my administrative schedule to include writing time. He was gracious and encouraged me on this project.

Both master's and D.Min. students who've given feedback as I've taught these strategies deserve thanks. Their input brought refinement. Faculty colleagues, especially Timothy Warren and John Reed, have given numerous valuable insights. Charles J. Stewart directed my doctoral studies at Purdue University. He allowed me to explore the matter of communication relevance in expository preaching and "refined" (to say the least) my thinking.

More praise than can be included in these brief pages goes to my wonderful wife, Denise. She nursed me back from a brain tumor, encouraged me to write, and, with quadrupled effort, managed our home in order to free me. To my children, Katie and David, I say a special "thank you" for letting me have those blocks of time in the study. It must have been very difficult for them to understand that "Daddy is at work now."

More generally, I am very grateful to Aubrey Malphurs and John Reed, who have mentored me and encouraged me to write. Haddon Robinson, too, has been an ongoing source of encouragement. I am grateful for his willingness to write the foreword. Several evaluators of early drafts of the manuscript refined the product: Gary Choong, Mike Ford, Scott Gibson, Sandi Glahn, and Timothy Warren gave valuable insights. I'm very grateful to my administrative assistants, Stephanie Folsom and Kristi Wilson, for their careful proofreading and for not laughing too much at my typing.

Introduction

ESSENTIAL READING

Like pizza, expository messages often come in two distinct forms: deep-dish, or thin and crispy. Either the content is so deep that we cannot possibly discern what we're really eating or the toppings are so sparse that, an hour later, we wonder why we bothered ordering. Deep-dish sermons are quite filling, even stuffy, with lots of chewing required. In contrast, thin and crispy sermons go down effortlessly, but they leave us craving more substance. Deep-dish sermons are full of stuff (after all, content rules!), while thin and crispy sermons appear very appetizing, though they offer little satisfaction.

Is it possible to deliver sermons that are both appetizing and satisfying? The answer is *yes!* Relevant biblical preaching not only tastes great, but it also satisfies the nutritional longings of the soul. Like a good recipe, however, relevant biblical preaching must mix the right ingredients in the correct proportions and sequence.

This book is not the first to address the topic of relevance. In their excellent books, Calvin Miller and Robert G. Duffett provide the case for relevant preaching.[1] In a much earlier work, Richard Halverson addresses the relevance of the Christian faith in the twentieth century.[2] More recently, Mark Galli and Brian Larson use a journalistic approach to discuss factors related to relevance in preaching.[3] David Henderson's *Culture Shift* provides an excellent assessment of the cultural elements that strongly influence preaching.[4]

None of these works, however, sets forth the strategies to achieve relevance in communication. Moreover, they do not specifically address expository preaching. In contrast, *Preaching with Relevance* develops ten strategies toward expository preaching that firmly root the message in the biblical text while demonstrating the relevance of the Scripture to daily living. These strategies grew out of my own doctoral research and from teaching homiletics at both the master's and doctoral level.

At the core of expository preaching are two questions for the preacher: (1) What does the text mean? (2) How do I communicate the relevance of the text's meaning to my listeners? *Preaching with Relevance* assumes that the preacher has answered the first question and then offers ten strategies to answer the second question. These strategies are no substitute for thorough exegesis and competent theology in expository preaching, and therefore are useless without substantive biblical content to communicate in the sermon.

Likewise, no strategy, or even exegesis or theology, can replace the preacher's relationship to God. Preaching from an empty spiritual life is about as valuable as honking your car horn when you're stuck behind an accident on the highway. I wholeheartedly agree with Calvin Miller's observation that every preacher needs to have an "Isaianic sign." Miller presents a forceful claim: "What is said must clearly communicate that we are Christians who speak for Christ. As the speech develops there must not be one sentence or one word which causes the hearer to doubt the force of our inner life in Christ."[5]

While this book will assist the preacher in achieving relevance in communication, these strategies are helps to those preachers who communicate God's Word with few reservations. The evangelical church seems to be long on technique and short on piety. I do not wish to add to the emphasis on technique.

Terms

My former composition teacher said, "Always define your terms." In this book, *communication relevance* refers to "the communicative link between the biblical content of the message and the listeners' lives so as to demonstrate pertinence or applicability of the biblical Truth."[6] I reserve the term *application* for the concrete beliefs, attitudes, values, and behaviors for which the sermon calls.

Relevance, however, must point the way to application. Thus, *relevance* is a larger term, closer in meaning to significance, bearing, or pertinence. Relevance includes more than application. Validity is an essential aim of communication relevance. In application, the listener asks "So what?" or "What difference does it make?"; in validity, the listener asks "Is it true?" or "Do I really buy that?" Thus, communication relevance includes both application and validity.

A Little Perspective

For a long time I, as both a preacher and a homiletician, resisted the push toward relevance. With only a cursory look, I rejected this orientation because it seemed too pragmatic and humanistic for my theocentric preaching paradigm. I hesitated because I feared that a focus on relevance would lead to what I think masquerades for appropriate biblical preaching. We hear sermons that are no more than pop-psychology ("Ten Timely Tips to Tame Your Teenager") or Sunday's weekly survival prescription ("How to Hold Up in a Fold-Up World"). These may be appealing and appropriate titles, but one could summarize the substance of truth found in some of those sermons on a three-by-five index card and still have white space.

I struggled with the push to "be relevant" because I focused on the wrong part of the communication process. I asked, "How can the *preacher* be relevant?" which is a focus on the *sender*. I also asked, "How can the *sermon* be relevant?" which is a focus on the *channel*. Moreover, I asked, "How can the *Bible* be relevant?" which is a focus on the *message*. But *relevance* is a conditional word. So we have to ask, "Relevant *to whom?*" which is a focus on the *receiver*.[7] At first, I feared that this receiver orientation would dilute biblical and theo-logical content, and that the sermon would simply become a sales job, having "qualified the customer." I therefore stress that we must take a communication perspective without rejecting the theological per-spective (the latter being that preaching ultimately seeks to bring glory to God through the glad submission of human hearts).[8]

Our communication perspective, then, serves as a means to convey the theological perspective. We are not *making* God's Word relevant, for it already *is* relevant. Surely, we who affirm the inspiration of Scripture believe that a God who initiated revelation of Himself, also believe that God's Word *is* relevant. The Bible's declaration of its relevance clarifies our belief: "All Scripture is God-breathed and is useful for teaching, rebuking, correcting and training in righteousness, so that the man of God may be thoroughly equipped for every good work" (2 Tim. 3:16–17).

While these verses do not suggest that the entire Bible is equally relevant or equally relevant at the same time, surely they claim that the Bible *is* relevant. We do not have to *make* the Bible relevant. Rather, our task is communication: We seek to *demonstrate* that God's Word is relevant. Hence, I believe that the pursuit of relevance in preaching is essentially communication relevance.

A Solid Foundation

Because we already have strong expository preaching primers, I won't repeat the foundations of expository preaching but rather as-sume a sermonic purpose and process for preaching. By this I mean a purpose and process that seeks to edify believers through careful "re-presentation" of the text(s) of Scripture as the A/author[9] intended it for the original readers, with application made for a specific preacher and audience.[10] I appreciate the insight of my colleague, John W. Reed, concerning the issue of relevance in expository preaching. Dr. Reed, after hearing Bill Hybels discuss his preaching philosophy in a 1989 pastors' conference, summarized,

Bill Hybels confesses that his problem in the church early in his ministry was its failure to be relevant. He built his ministry on relevant topical preaching. It is possible that he might have been just as successful if he had included in his preaching relevant expository sermons. The issue is not the *topical* preaching but the *relevance.* Many individuals have rejected expository preaching because the preachers they heard had never been discipled in the real thing.[11]

I have the privilege of interacting with about ten pastors per week. Regularly they say to me, "People just don't seem to want to listen to good, solid Bible preaching. Yet, they crave the things that only the Bible can give them." Or they ask, "When my messages have far more life-changing substance, why do people flock to that church that just preaches fluff?" Paul's familiar warning to Timothy echoes in my mind: "For the time will come when men will not put up with sound doctrine. Instead, to suit their own desires, they will gather around them a great number of teachers to say what their itching ears want to hear" (2 Tim. 4:3).

I'm not a prophet, so I'm not going to argue that the day has arrived, but it seems that we're getting dangerously close. This book is not about preaching for itching ears. It's about preaching substantive biblical truth in a way that people can discern its relevance for their lives as they seek to walk with God. I am convinced that we do not have to sacrifice biblical content to speak to our culture or various contemporary cultures, despite some of the claims (unsubstantiated, I might add) about attention spans and learning styles of various generations. Greg Laurie offers this colorful insight:

> When I preach, do I springboard from the Word or into the Word? The Bible shouldn't just be our diving board; it should be our destination—the pool where we spend the most time.[12]

Countless interactions with preachers asking for useful strategies to communicate the relevance of God's Word prompted the writing of this book. It is toward this goal that I believe we can preach relevant biblical (expository) sermons without dumbing down the content.

Consequently, this is a book of strategies—namely, ethical plans of action—not gimmicks or manipulation. If you want a how-to book of communication gimmicks, this book is not for you. But if you want tested and accepted strategies, then keep reading.

Preview

As mentioned above, this book describes (and prescribes) ten strategies to take the sermon from the exegeted text to communication relevance with listeners.[13] Toward that end, each chapter includes a general objective as well as specific objectives to guide the reader. Perhaps even more important is the inclusion of a section entitled "You Try It!" As I've taught these ten strategies to seasoned pastors, I've seen "the lights come on" as they disciplined themselves to work through these brief exercises. So I encourage you to add a few minutes to your reading of the chapter and take advantage of the "You Try It!" section.

1

Look from the Pew's Perspective

The *general objective* in this chapter is to grasp the receiver-orientation essential for understanding communication relevance.

The *specific objectives* in this chapter are

1. to see the value of knowing the people to whom we preach,
2. to become familiar with a tool for analyzing or getting to know the audience to whom we preach.

In relevant biblical preaching, perspective is everything. When it comes to relevance, we must ask ourselves, "Who determines whether the sermon is relevant?"[1] From a strictly *theological* perspective, the only viable answer is *God*. The Lord did not leave us His Word in hopes that we would discover some human utilitarian value in it. He revealed Himself and His will to bring glory to Himself through the obedience and praise of His people.

From a communication perspective, however, *listeners* determine whether the sermon is relevant. We might think that this communication perspective seems contrary to the theological perspective, but the two are quite compatible. If we did not believe that God's Word *is* relevant, why would we attempt to *demonstrate* that it is?

If, then, we are to demonstrate the relevance of God's Word to listeners, we must take the perspective of the pew rather than the pulpit. As a student of Scripture, trained in exegesis and theology, I can "get lost" in the study of the Ancient Near East's worship of Baal, the composition of the tribes of Israel, or the debates about James' theology. As a preacher, give me good biblical-historical-theological evidence, and I'll buy the sermon's big idea or homiletical proposition.

In doing so, I'm thinking as a preacher because I'm living in a preacher's world. The people to whom I speak on Saturday night and Sunday morning live in a world of bioethics, violence, car payments, sitcoms, and dot-coms. Trying to explain to them Elijah's conflict on Mount Carmel (1 Kings 18) by giving an abbreviated history lesson on Baal worship is like trying to sell flood insurance in the desert. That's because I'm talking in the preacher's world.

When I talk in the listener's world, I may need to state the essential tenets of Baal worship so that people will understand what Elijah was up against. For example, I may say something along the lines of

> The ancient Near East offered an assortment of deities. People could choose one god over another, or to be safe, they might worship several gods. Elijah made it perfectly clear that the people could not waver between gods. The God of Israel is the only true God, Elijah claimed.

Sitting in the pew are Jay and Leah. Their son Jason is a sophomore this year at a major university. One of his classes is a study of world religions. Jay and Leah fear what's being pumped into Jason's mind. He hears that religion is a sociological phenomenon of every culture, a matter of choice, one option in pluralism. Thus, his professor argues, to suggest that there is only one correct belief system is irrational and exclusive.

Such are the culture wars of our day. They sound a lot like the wars of Elijah's day. When we see the similarity between the two situations, we need to ask, "Why was Elijah so insistent that the people of Israel not waver between gods?" And when we discover the answer in the theology of the Old Testament, we are ready to talk to Jay and Leah about how to help Jason face the challenges of his own culture wars. When I look from the pulpit, I see Baal worship, Elijah, sinful Israel, and a fascinating showdown on Mount Carmel. When I look from the pew, I see Jason, 230 miles away, shy, questioning, tempted, and facing the challenges to his monotheistic Christian faith. And I see his parents, who fear for his mind and heart. I also see a relevant answer in God's Word to Jason's struggle. In relevant biblical preaching, perspective is everything.

If we are going to demonstrate the relevance of God's Word to our listeners, we must look from the perspective of the pew. That look begins with acquainting ourselves with those to whom we speak. Hence, the remainder of this chapter delineates a tool for audience analysis.[2] Before moving to that tool, however, let me share Pastor Ray Pritchard's insightful words:

> Everyone has a story to tell, even the people who seem to smile all the time. This is one of the first things a young pastor learns when he graduates from seminary and begins his ministry. Some people look so well-adjusted and happy that you think they don't have a care in the world. But they do. If you work with people long enough, you discover that even the "perfect" people know all about sorrow and heartache.[3]

The seasoned pastor preaches from the vantage of the shepherd who knows the sheep. The pastor's analysis will happen somewhat intuitively and in an ongoing fashion. Nevertheless, as I have heard frequently from Doctor of Ministry students, many of them seasoned pastors, "This analysis [tool] opened my eyes to see my people in ways I had not thought about." It's amazing how differently we preach to people when we learn about their hurtful childhood, the tyranny they're under at work, or the loneliness they feel because of neglect from a spouse.

Consider Bill Hybels' insight: "If we're going to speak with integrity to secular men and women, we need to work through two critical areas before we step into the pulpit. . . . The first is to *understand the way they think*. . . . The second prerequisite to effective preaching to non-Christians is that we *like them*."[4]

To analyze our audience, we need to analyze generally, theologically, psychologically, demographically, and with the preaching purpose in view. The following section provides a tool for audience analysis. When I preach as a guest speaker, I use a much-abbreviated version of this tool. At a minimum, it gives me a glimpse of the people to whom I'll be speaking. Otherwise, I arrive clueless.

To the preacher who regularly speaks in one setting, however, I, like the IRS, recommend that the preacher use the "long form" at least once per year. (This is where any similarity between the IRS and me stops!) Following the Tool for Audience Analysis, the chapter will provide sample Application Grids. Keeping an Application Grid on my desk during the homiletical phase of my preparation is a simple way to keep the people before me. If I'm not intentional about doing so, I may slip back into my perspective of looking from the pastor's study or the pulpit instead of looking from the pew. Remember that the analysis is not of the entire church body but only of the preaching audience.

Tool for Audience Analysis

Instructions: Complete the following outline for audience analysis by reading and applying the recommendations and answering (where appropriate) the questions. Record the sources for your conclusions, even if anecdotal.

Plan to Analyze Your Audience(s)

This first phase of the analysis is general and allows us to gather general information about the community and culture from a variety of resources.

1. Plan to analyze generally.
   a. Various national polls provide general analyses of audiences.
      • George Gallup, *Religion in America, 50 Years: 1935–1985* (Princeton, NJ: Gallup Organization, 1985)

- *Journal of Adult Training* 2, no. 1 (1989)
- *Journal of Adult Training* 3, no. 2 (1991)

b. Sociological and cultural studies provide general analyses of audiences.

- John Naisbitt and Patricia Aburdene, *Megatrends 2000* (New York: Morrow, 1990)
- James Patterson and Peter Kim, *The Day America Told the Truth* (New York: Prentice-Hall Press, 1991)
- George Barna, *America 2000* (Glendale, CA: Barna Research Group, 1989); *The Frog in the Kettle* Ventura, CA: Regal, 1990); *User Friendly Churches (Ventura, CA:* Regal, 1991)
- David Henderson, *Culture-Shift* (Grand Rapids: Baker, 1998)

Note: Use all sources critically. Be careful not to read *descriptive* research as *prescriptive*.

Too many preachers stop at cultural analysis. Cultural analysis is valuable, but insufficient by itself. It's valuable to know the general "gatekeepers" of information and trends in a given culture, but people are still individuals who have made choices about their values and beliefs. Likewise, churches are communities that often take on a subculture or traits of their own. Hence, we must go beyond cultural analysis.

2. Plan to analyze locally.

a. Chamber of Commerce analyses provide local information about audiences.

b. Compuserve's® "Go Neighbor" zip code survey provides local analyses of audiences.

c. Several databases of local information are available via the Internet.

d. Most towns or cities have a Web site.

3. Plan to analyze particularly.

a. Analyze a particular audience through records, questionnaires, surveys, visitation of all kinds, personal observations, informal conversations, past experience, pre-sermon discussions, post-sermon discussions, and so on.

b. Talk to people; listen to people!

4. Learn about and *love* your audience.
5. Pray for your audience.
   a. Keep an active prayer list of your audience and pray through that list on a regular basis.
   b. Stop the sermon preparation process at the point of audience analysis and, from the pulpit, pray through the empty seats by visualizing the audience and individuals who will listen. Or at least create an Application Grid with people's names so that you can pray by visualizing them. A sample Application Grid appears at the end of this chapter.

Theological Analysis

1. Identify your audience's spiritual condition(s) by percentages.

Unregenerate
__% of the people are far from the kingdom (maybe some interest).
__% of the people are coming to the kingdom (seekers).
__% of the people are near the kingdom (contemplative seekers).

Regenerate
__% of the people seem to be immature or carnal.
__% of the people seem to be immature and growing.
__% of the people seem to be maturing but stagnant.
__% of the people seem to be maturing steadily.

2. Identify your audience's spiritual longings.
__% of the audience longs for transcendence (the urge to *be*).
__% of the audience longs for action (the urge to *do*).
__% of the audience longs for community (the urge to *belong*).

Psychological Analysis

1. How does the audience *think* (process information)?

Does the audience follow the reflective thinking process of (1) recognizing a felt need or difficulty, (2) defining the problem, (3) collecting and analyzing data, (4) listing alternative solutions, (5) identifying criteria for a solution, and (6) adopting a solution? Does the audience follow this process closely? Does it follow some other process of "thinking" (authority, tradition, spontaneity, rational-emotive, anecdotal, and so on)?

2. How does the audience *feel* (sense experience)?

3. How does the audience *act* (choose from different options)?

4. Identify the audience's paradigms.
   a. What are the audience's attitudes? (Attitudes answer the question "How do you think, feel, and act concerning . . . ?")
   b. What are the audience's beliefs? (Beliefs answer the question "How strongly do you think, feel, and act concerning . . . ?" or "What do you embrace?")
   c. What are the audience's values? (Values answer the question "What do you hold dear?")

Demographic Analysis

1. What percent of the audience is ages
   ___ 5–12 ___ 13–18 ___ 19–22 ___ 23–30 ___ 31–40 ___ 41–55
   ___ 56–65 ___ 66–80 ___ over 80

2. What percent is
   ___ male ___ female

3. What is the approximate mean adult annual income? (Take an anonymous survey, if necessary.)
   $_____ annually

4. What percent of the audience lives
   ___ within one mile of the church property ___ 1–5 miles
   ___ 6–10 miles ___ over 10 miles

5. What percent is
   ___ Caucasian ___ Hispanic ___ African American
   ___ Native American ___ other _____

6. What percent works in
   ___ "white collar" occupations ___ "blue collar" occupations
   ___ unemployed

7. What percent is
   ___ married ___ divorced ___ never married
   ___ divorced and remarried ___ widowed

8. What percent identifies with
   ___ a particular political viewpoint or party

9. What percent in regard to education has:
   ___ no high school diploma ___ high school or equivalent
   ___ college ___ graduate degree

10. What percent has been Christian
    ___ less than 1 year ___ over 3 years ___over 5 years
    ___ over 10 years ___ over 20 years ___ never

11. What percent has
    ___ "grown up in church"
    ___ started coming to this church within the last two years
    ___ started coming to this church within the last five years

12. What percent comes from backgrounds that are predominantly
    ___ unchurched ___ Catholic ___ Mainline Protestant
    ___ Evangelical ___ non-Christian religion

Purpose-Oriented Analysis

1. Are any members of the audience "hostile" (argumentative, adverse to Christian beliefs, application, and so on)? Or are any members of this audience "hostile" to this sermon's purpose? If so, why?

   _____

   _____

   _____

2. What feedback has been received from audience members about previous sermons?

_____

_____

_____

3. How long should sermons be for this audience? (Is length a significant issue?)

_____

_____

_____

4. Have previous messages delivered to this audience been generally positive, negative, corrective-admonishing, encouraging, motivational, instructive, and so on? How might previous sermons influence future messages?

_____

_____

_____

5. Are there significant "issues" that undermine or influence the overall ministry (a split, unresolved tensions, financial concerns, tensions between the preacher and audience members, etc.)?

_____

_____

_____

6. What will stimulate interest in the sermon's subject for this audience?

_____

_____

_____

7. In what ways does this audience influence the organization (structure, outline) of a sermon?

_____

_____

8. What is impossible to know in advance of preaching to this audience?

_____

_____

_____

9. What do you like about preaching to this audience/in this setting?

_____

_____

_____

10. What do you dislike about preaching to this audience/in this setting?

_____

_____

_____

Adaptation to Audience

Become aware of the segments within your audience. Within every audience there are small groups who are different from the many individuals or from the audience as a whole. Selectively address segments within the audience. As in exegesis of the text, not every detail of your exegesis of the audience will show up in every sermon. Enough messages are selectivity addressed to the various segments of the audience, however, to enable the message to hit home to a large percentage of "real" people.

Additionally, think in terms of community as well as individuals. Most of the information gleaned from the above Audience Analysis tool will inform you about individuals. But sometimes we have a text that applies to the body as well as the individual. Thus, the sermon needs to develop a corporate application as well as an application for individuals.

Adapt to the audience in some simple ways, as necessary, to aid communication:

- Dress—semi-formal, casual, or sporty?
- Language—elevated, normal, or conversational?
- Arguments—logical, ethical, or emotional?
- Arrangement—deductive, inductive, conceptual, imagery, and so on?
- Support—credible authorities, research, statistics, illustrations?
- Allusions/images—biblical, historical, current, or local?
- Association/dissociation with audience?

Sample Application Grids

On the following pages are sample Aapplication Grids that provide a way of "keeping the people in front of you" as you prepare. The first grid is a four-column grid of names that represent somewhat of a cross-section of the congregation. The following guidelines will help you to use the grid for maximum value.

Guidelines

a. As you think through the flow of the message, look at the names on the Application Grid and ask, "How will this truth touch this person?"

b. Ask, "How should this person respond in terms of belief, attitude, values, or behavior?"

c. Aim to be concrete, but shape application in terms that are general enough not to identify or embarrass anyone.

d. Don't be so specific with application that you become irrelevant. (If application gets too narrow, it may miss a large percentage of the people, who will then think, "That's not me." More importantly, it may "misrepresent" the text.)

e. Change the names on the grid monthly, especially if you preach to one audience regularly.

Sam	Kate	Mark	Bill
Suzanne	Lucy	Tim	Rex
Margaret	Harold	Paul	David
Beth	Marcia	Phil	Stephen
Cindy	Dale	Janet	Gary
Jim	Sandy	Debra	Wayne
Joan	Chuck	Ralph	Shirley
Ho Chin	Megan	Gabe	Beverley
Sherri	Al	Carol	Allen
Richard	Lynne	Bill	Sally
Tommy	Heather	Jay	LaTeisa

If you cannot use a grid with specific names, or if you want to focus on a specific group or a specific situation, adapt your grid by plugging in categories similar to those on the grids below.

	Home	Work	School	Church	Subculture
Children					
Single					
Married					
Widowed					
Divorced					

	Self-employed	Employed	Work part time	Work on commission	Retired
Male Children					
Single Men					
Married Men					
Widowed Men					
Divorced Men					

Conclusion

I know one preacher who places a collage of pictures from his congregation in front of him as he prepares each message. Whatever the tool—an application grid of names or a collage of pictures—know the people to whom you will speak so that you can prepare from the pew's perspective, for in preaching with relevance, perspective is everything.

YOU TRY IT!

1. Use the Tool for Audience Analysis presented in this chapter to analyze *your* audience.
2. Develop an Application Grid for *your* audience.
3. Decide what adaptations to your audience may be appropriate.

2

Get into a Good Argument

The *general objective* in this chapter is to understand the value of rhetorical argumentation as the paradigm for communication relevance. The *specific objectives* in this chapter are

1. to translate knowledge of the audience into message content that will function as evidence to support the message's central claim;
2. to learn to use the Audience Relevance Worksheet as a tool for establishing communication relevance.

Having analyzed the audience, we have a pretty good idea about how life looks from the pew. How, then, do we craft the specifics of the sermon so that our listeners will understand the meaning of the passage(s), affirm the sermon's homiletical big idea, and apply the sermon's truth in their lives? More specifically, how do we choose supporting material? How much explanation of the text is enough? How much explanation is too much?

For every sermon, the preacher must make selections. Some things are selected "in"; some are selected "out." It's neither necessary nor wise to include in one message everything we have studied. When we ask ourselves about what material to select, we're really asking ourselves, "For this audience, how do I *advance the claim* of this sermon?" Or to maintain the receiver orientation, "What evidence will help my listeners *accept the claim* of this message?"

In asking ourselves these questions as part of our sermon preparation, we quickly discern that every sermon is an argument that seeks to advance a claim through supporting evidence. Thus, we think of argumentation as communication. Argumentation is a subset of persuasion, but unlike some successful means of persuasion, argumentation requires that receivers (in preaching, listeners) accept the justification of our claim.

The perspective of argumentation as communication implies that instead of being interested in the forms of arguments—as in formal logic—we are concerned primarily with their function. Thus, a second implication of this perspective of argumentation as communication is that we will not be concerned with following rules of argumentation but with the ways in which people actually do argue. More specifically, we're interested in the ways in which people actually accept claims. (Very few people parse a sermon, seeking to discover the parts of an oral syllogism, but careful listeners do require *acceptable* evidence to support the sermon's claim.)[1]

Sermons make claims on our lives. A good homiletical proposition, which grows from an exegetical proposition and a theological proposition (see chap. 4), makes a claim on people's lives. So when our exegetical and theological work is complete in our preparation, we need to ask ourselves, "What evidence will help my listeners accept the claim of this message?" Note, selecting evidence is part of our *preparation* rather than the eventual homiletical product. In other words, we probably will not structure the sermon as a deductive argument and state the elements explicitly:

Claim (homiletical proposition or big idea)

- ▶   I. Evidence
- ▶   II. More evidence
- ▶   III. More evidence

This may be an acceptable structure for some sermons, but as will be seen in chapter 4, sermons take shape for other reasons, and the "parts" of the argument will be integrated into that shape. The point here is to understand that we are not yet interested in the overall structure (shape, arrangement, form) of the sermon. We are interested in how the sermon is perceived *by listeners* as an argument that advances a claim. Thus, once the exegetical and theological work is complete and I move to homiletical preparation, I must ask myself some questions. Before moving to those questions, however, some definitions of the terms of argumentation will be helpful.

Language (the words and sentences we use) can function in several ways in argumentation as communication:

1. *Claim:* A statement that we wish to have accepted by a receiver, but that we find is somehow challenged. A claim is not merely a statement. A statement is simply an assertion or a proposition. Any statement can, of course, become a claim, if our statement is challenged. In preaching, the sermon's claim is the homiletical proposition or big idea. Our sermon's claim is usually not explicitly or audibly challenged, but every sermon's claim is challenged implicitly by human depravity. Examples:

   a. *Speaker:*   You should eat more vegetables. (= statement = readily accepted)

      Receiver: What good are vegetables? (statement becomes a claim)

   b. *Speaker:*   The president is a great leader. (statement)

      Receiver: That all depends on how you define "great." (statement becomes a claim)

   c. *Speaker:*   God is always gracious to His children. (statement)

      Receiver: But what about my husband, who suffers with bone cancer? (statement becomes a claim)

2. *Evidence:* Language that functions to express an idea that is already acceptable or evident to receiver(s), and thereby appears to support the claim.

Evidence can come in a variety of forms. It is crucial that something identified as "evidence" functions for the *listener(s)* as grounds to strengthen the claim. Typically, for evidence to function as such requires that the language is already "evident" to the receiver(s). This means that evidence is not simply cold, cognitive facts. Sometimes (perhaps even often) a heart-tugging story functions as evidence. The point is that evidence comes in a variety of forms. The key is *function*, not form.

Speaker:	God is always gracious in His actions.
	What might function for you as evidence to support that claim?
Receiver 1:	God is holy and cannot do anything unholy.
Receiver 2:	Even when God punishes, He is merciful.
Receiver 3:	When I sin, God is merciful to forgive me, even though I commit some of the same sins over and over again.

Notice that in the example above, I asked, "What might function *for you* as evidence?" So at some point the sermon probably works with potential evidence. Some evidence may be stated explicitly, as in the following example from a sermon manuscript.

When I was thinking through the implications of this message, I was, at first troubled by the word *always*. I thought, *Is God always gracious in His actions? What about that terrible earthquake in Mexico? What about the person who is stricken with a terrible, maybe even fatal, disease at the age of forty?*

As I thought through different situations, I came to the realization that God's will is always the silver lining in the cloud. Even in cases of extreme personal suffering, if God is working His plan to strengthen our faith, His plan is more loving and more perfect for conforming to the image of His Son than any path we might choose. There are times that I would choose another path, but God loves me more than I love myself, and I'm thankful that He knows what I need to become more like Him.

I've shared with you a little in the past about my good friends, Annie and Tommy. Annie and Tommy are retirement age now. For most of their forty-eight years of marriage, Annie has been in a wheelchair or so shriveled from arthritis that she could not even take care of personal hygiene without Tommy's aid. When I was their pastor, I would stop in to try to encourage them. By the time I left their house, I was the one who was encouraged. I heard them talk about their love for Jesus and how years of a slower pace (than most people) have allowed them to read God's Word and pray and talk together. No, they would never have selected such a path, but looking back, they wouldn't have missed it. God is *always* gracious in His actions.

Evidence may come in the form of successful application of God's Word, as in the example above. (We'll consider "success stories" in more detail in chap. 8.) For others, evidence may need to be a statistic, an example from the preacher's personal experience, a Bible verse, or a true story from a respected Christian publication. Evidence will take a variety of forms because listeners are different and they make different demands. Some claims require more evidence than others. What matters is that we continue to look from the perspective of the pew so that we can offer evidence acceptable to the *listeners,* not the speaker. That's how to develop argumentation as communication; that is, that's how to get into a good argument. But sometimes we need to show how the evidence connects for people. In other words, what warrants this evidence?

3. *Warrant:* Words that demonstrate the connection between the evidence and the claim.

Claim:	God is gracious in His actions
Evidence:	God is holy and cannot do anything unholy.
Receiver:	What does God's holiness have to do with His gracious actions?
Warrant:	Because of God' pure, holy character, we can trust Him to deal with us as He has dealt with people in the past. Even in cases of judgment, we can discern God's grace.

4. *Qualifier:* Language that reveals how confident we are in the claim.

Qualifier:	God is gracious in His actions, but He is also just; so sometimes He must bring judgment in the form of wrath. Still, ninety-nine times out of a hundred, God is more than gracious. Realizing how gracious God really is might require simply getting the right perspective, like Joseph did.

5. *Reservation:* Language that functions to demonstrate what circumstance may make us retract our claim altogether. If we are stating absolute truths of God's Word as our claim, we will not need reservations. If our claim is more like a proverb (an observation rather than a promise), we may need reservations to help some people accept our claim.

Claim:	It's better to acquire a small amount honestly than to acquire great wealth dishonestly.
Evidence:	I knew a man who embezzled thousands of dollars from his father's business. On the outside, he had a beautiful home, drove nice cars, was respected in the community, and appeared to be "ahead of the game." At home, he was enslaved to alcohol. He could not live with himself for what he had done to his father. So, in misery, he tried to drink away his guilty conscience.
Reservation:	It's better to acquire a small amount honestly than to acquire great wealth dishonestly, *unless you only care about how things look on the outside.*

With the terminology of argumentation in view, the preacher is ready to ask the argumentative questions:

1. What might the audience demand as evidence to support the claim (for example, biblical data, examples from life, personal illustrations, statistics, success stories, etc.)?

2. What are the connecting ideas, the warrants, between the claim and the evidence?

3. Does the audience need qualifiers or reservations?

I find it helpful to keep an Audience Relevance Worksheet on my desk as I begin the homiletical stage of my preparation.

Audience Relevance Worksheet

1. State the major claim (or homiletical big idea) being advanced.

2. Ask yourself, What might the *audience* demand as evidence to support the claim (for example, biblical data, examples from life, personal illustrations, statistics, success stories, etc.)?

3. Ask yourself, What are the warrants, the connecting ideas between the claim and the evidence?

4. Does the audience need qualifiers or reservations?

Conclusion

What matters is that we continue to look from the perspective of the pew so that we can answer these questions with language acceptable to the *listeners,* not the speaker. That's how we get into a good argument!

YOU TRY IT!

Read the following excerpt from an expository message. Identify the sentence that appears to function as the big idea or claim and the sentences that appear to function as evidence. (The sentences are numbered for your convenience.)

[1]Thus, God alone can show us that there is only one true God.
[2]No wonder He commanded us to have no other gods before

Him. [3]Not only did He defeat the idols of Baal, but only the God of Israel has conquered death through the sacrificial death of His son, Jesus. [4]All the prophets or the so-called gods of various religions cannot do what Jesus can do. [5]When the roll is called at Muhammad's grave, he must say "Here." [6]When Joseph Smith's name is called, he must respond, "Here." [7]When Buddha's name is called, he must respond, "Present." [8]But when Jesus' name is called, we hear silence, and then comes an explanation: "He is not here; He is risen!"

Claim = sentence # ＿＿＿＿

Evidence = sentences # ＿＿＿＿＿＿＿＿＿＿＿＿＿＿＿＿＿

3

Whet an Appetite for God's Word

The *general objective* in this chapter is to see the significance of the sermon's introduction for demonstrating the sermon as relevant to listeners.

The *specific objectives* in this chapter are

1. to learn how to develop the essential elements of relevant sermon introductions;
2. to observe an example, with analysis, of a relevant introduction.

I'd love to think that Jay and Leah came to church this morning craving the truth of God's Word about monotheism. Perhaps they did, but they may not know it yet. If I begin the message by taking them to the ancient Near East or by talking about the great victory of Elijah, they probably will overlook the relevance of God's Word. I cannot assume their appetites for God's Word have been whetted simply because I've said, "Let's turn in our Bibles to First Kings 18." I have to help them *want* to hear from God.

Rather than assume that people will discern the relevance of the biblical passage, the sermon needs to begin where people are and then *create an appetite* for God's Word. Kenneth Burke, the leading rhetorical-cultural critic of the twentieth century, explained his communication theory of form: "Form is the creation of an appetite in the mind of an auditor [listener], and the adequate satisfaction of that appetite."[1] Referring to the pizza analogy in the introduction to this book, the sermon's introduction must supply the fragrance of fresh-baked pizza in the oven with the promise of satisfaction when one has completed the meal. Of course, the sermon must deliver what its introduction promises. (See chap. 5 for the concept of unity in the sermon.) So the sermon will start by talking about how we know that we really have the truth. We'll probe questions such as

> Is there only one God? Are we being too narrow-minded, or intolerant, when we contend that the God of the Bible is the only true God? Why can we be confident that Christianity is right?

More than merely probing these questions in a cognitive way, the sermon needs to touch the heart and show the significance of these questions in concrete experience. I may try to show, for example, the significance of teaching our children that there is one true God rather than a smorgasbord of religious options. I may then move back to teaching our children the truth about God; to do so we must be convinced that God is who He claims to be. At this point, Jay and Leah should be thinking about Jason and feeling the tension that begs for relief, relief that only God's Word can supply. I may even say,

> Those of you who are parents may be concerned about the things your kids hear in school. We cannot play "Christmas carols." We can play only "holiday music." I appreciate that the public school is an institution of the state and cannot be involved in the establishment of a single religion, but your kids who do not understand such matters may get mixed messages.

When I move, then, from talking about religious options and teaching children about God to the showdown on Mount Carmel, they are eager to hear about Elijah's contest. Why? Because I've shown them *what's at stake for them* in this message.[2] Once we look from the pew and whet people's appetite for God's Word, we are ready to show people what God's truth looks like "on the street." The remainder of this chapter delineates how to shape the sermon's introduction for communication relevance, to whet the listener's appetite for God's Word.

Surely, preachers should aim for variety, especially those who preach regularly to the same congregation. Yet there are nine basic steps, or elements, involved in all relevant introductions.

Steps to Shape Relevant Sermon Introductions

In using the term *steps*, I don't mean to suggest that every introduction should follow this sequence. Every introduction should, however, include all nine elements. The following sequence of steps is what helps me to think through the "rhetorical logic" of what I want to accomplish in the introduction.

1. Begin with the People

All that was presented in chapter 1 on the perspective of the audience is fundamental to this first element in introducing the sermon. Stated as a principle, beginning with the people could be stated like this: _Preaching is talking to people about themselves from the Bible rather than talking about the Bible._ So begin by talking to people directly about what's going on in their lives. A personal comment or two may build rapport.

This is not a time to lose time. Don't ease into the introduction so gradually that your first statements either do not relate to the sermon or they let people know not to listen until about your fifth or sixth sentence. (The exception to this is the guest speaker who should build a little rapport with the audience through his or her opening words.)

Sometimes a very direct statement that aims at application of the subject will gain attention as well as immediately show the listeners the relevance of the message to their lives. One preacher began his sermon by saying, "I read in the newspaper this week that eighty percent of all married men in this country will cheat on their wives at least once during their marriage. And I suppose that there are men in this congregation who have contributed to that statistic." Too startling? Perhaps. I'm sure he had the audience's attention, though. And for a message on the subject of marital fidelity, he got a rabbit start on relevance.

2. Evoke an Emotional/Spiritual Image

A single, concrete image repeated throughout the sermon, if not overused, has the power to unify, clarify, and give precision to the sermon. Centuries ago, Aristotle described the power of metaphorical language:

> It is a great thing, indeed, to make a proper use of these poetical forms [unknown expression in the common language], as also of compounds and strange words. But the greatest thing by far is to be a master of metaphor. It is the one thing that cannot be learnt from others; and it is also a sign of genius, since a good metaphor implies an intuitive perception of the similarity in dissimilars.[3]

Metaphor still holds the same power of immediate connection and sustained clarity. Because of the connection acquired through metaphor, the repeated or extended metaphor or image sustains momentum throughout the sermon, while also providing unity and clarity.

In a Christmas-season sermon entitled "God with Us in Time," Pastor Steve Stroope opened by telling that he had offered to bring a food item to a family reunion. His mother told him to bring a green vegetable. Pastor Steve continued:

> Being the cook I am, I stopped in at the local [restaurant] and ordered a spinach soufflé. When I looked at the spinach soufflé, I realized that it was near the bottom of the pan, and they would have to bring me a new one, or it wouldn't be enough to take to the dinner. The person behind the counter warned me that it

would be ten to twenty minutes before it would be ready. "Fine," I said, "I'll wait." This apparently surprised them because people usually do not want to wait for their food at [this restaurant]. But I stood there patiently. They offered me mashed potatoes, with gravy even, but I explained that I wanted only the spinach soufflé. Now, I like mashed potatoes, maybe even better than I like spinach soufflé, but mashed potatoes aren't green; at least, not good ones. For this occasion, only spinach soufflé would do. No imitations! No substitutes!

Unfortunately, there are lots of people out there who are offering us mashed potatoes. But the real Emmanuel is worth waiting for. For this occasion, only He will do.[4]

Throughout the sermon, then, Pastor Steve asked, "Is that just mashed potatoes they're offering you?" Or he commented, "That's not the Christ child born in Bethlehem; that's just mashed potatoes." He concluded by saying, "Mashed potatoes seem desirous, but they just won't cut it when only spinach soufflé will do. When Jesus came the first time, it was worth the wait. When He comes the second time, it will be worth the wait. Be careful of the mashed potatoes. Wait for the spinach!"

Some might be tempted to think, *That's hokey,* or *What a trite gimmick!* But the force communicated by the single, concrete image brings clarity as only the power of metaphor can. Warren Wiersbe captures it in his "usual exceptional" fashion:

What's supposed to happen to you when you hear a metaphor? If the metaphor is merely embellishment ("He was as frustrated as a termite in a yo-yo") you might think to yourself, "Now, wasn't that clever!" But that kind of response turns the metaphor into a distraction instead of discovery. Instead of focusing on *what's* being said, you start paying more attention to how it's being said; and that kind of response can be lethal to good communication.

If the metaphor is "dead" ("He's a bull in a china shop"), you might groan inwardly and perhaps even turn the speaker off. But if the metaphor is alive and vivid ("Why have you made me your target?" [Job 7:20]), you will probably find yourself *connecting* and saying to yourself, "I see something! I feel something! I understand something!"[5]

Thus, a single image serves to unify the sermon and communicate its message with greater clarity and precision. Perhaps the most critical step in a sermon introduction that begins with the people is to develop the listener's need for the sermon.

3. Develop the Listener's Need

Introductions must tell listeners what's at stake for them in the sermon, that is, how this sermon will speak to a particular need in their lives. Because people often do not "come to preaching" with the need that will be addressed by the sermon on their minds, we may have to help them feel that particular need. (See chap. 7 for a discussion of the process of adjusting the questions.) No preacher can possibly speak to all the identified needs in most audiences. In fact, why would any preacher want to speak to identified (or felt) needs only? (Chap. 7 will address the matter of "felt needs" more fully.) The Bible speaks to needs that are far more significant than most of the needs that people have identified in their lives. If we probe a little, people will adjust their thinking to more significant needs, the kind that sermons should address. As John Piper proclaims, "People are starving for the grandeur of God and the vast majority do not know it."[6] So we must raise the need that the message will address and develop that need a bit so that people think about and feel that need. In developing the listener's need, we will touch upon the subject of the sermon, but we must be very intentional in stating and clarifying the narrower subject of the sermon.

4. Move from the People to the Subject

Every sermon introduction needs to identify the subject and *show* people why this subject is relevant for them. Some introductions introduce the entire big idea or homiletical proposition, and others may lead into the first major move of the message, but at the very least, when the introduction is complete, listeners need to know the sermon's *subject*—what is going to be talked about (what the text is talking about). This subject is narrow rather than a broad topic. The sermon is not, for example, on the subject of "prayer" but rather on the subject of "how to pray through a crisis."

5. Give a Sneak Peak at the Point

Coinciding with showing people what's at stake and without tipping your hand, probe the subject enough to show people what lines of application they can anticipate. Most people listen for "the take." They ask, "What am I going to *get* out of this?" That may not be the most worshipful or theocentric question, but unless we have some rhetorical sensitivity to that question, our sermon probably never leaves the rafters to arrive in the pew.

6. Create an Appetite for the Sermon

What we really want to create an appetite for is God's Word—the sermon's text. It is hoped that the expository message will so accurately reflect the text that the sermon and the text are nearly inseparable. Whether the sermon will be developed deductively or inductively, shape the introduction into one of the following:

- a question to be answered
- an issue to be explored
- a problem to be solved
- a situation to be resolved

The remainder of the sermon then answers the question or solves the problem, which, as chapter 5 will discuss, unifies the sermon and delivers what the introduction promises.

7. Connect the Sermon to the Text

Before announcing the text's reference and before reading the passage, provide context or enough background so that the passage can be understood in its original context. Structure the sermon, and explain, "As we study this passage together, we'll discover the answer to our question [the solution to our problem, or so forth]."

- State that the text you're going to read deals with this same subject that you've been talking about.
- Be sure to promise only what the sermon can deliver.

Do not assume that your listeners know *why* you turn their attention to the Bible. You must give them *warrant* (a connection to the subject of the introduction) for looking at the passage. Otherwise, the text may simply be a *non sequitur* to everything that you've already said (the need and the subject). What you want is just the opposite. You want your introductory words to whet an appetite for the text of Scripture.

8. Read the Text with Expression

It is unfortunate that some people read the Bible like the radio announcer reads the commodities report—monotone, no emotion, no variety in pitch, punch, or pace.[7] The Bible is alive and relevant. How can anyone read Saul's chase of David as if it were without suspense or drama? The play-by-play of a no-hitter would sound more exciting. Even a very logical section of an epistle should be read with the emotion of a loving apostle writing to his spiritual children. (If we consider context and historical occasion, there's a story in that epistle!)

9. Ensure a Clean Start

Before moving to the first major move of the body of the sermon, briefly review the "lay of the land" from the introduction. Repeat the narrowed subject. Repeat the focus question (question, issue, problem, or situation). (Chap. 7 will develop further the strategy of raising the focus question for the sermon.) Preview the sermon's structure that will provide the answer. The remainder of the sermon then gives the answer, resolution, or solution.

If the sermon is to develop deductively, the preacher will state the entire big idea or homiletical proposition, thus answering the focus question before moving to the first major move of the sermon. The remainder of the sermon then works to validate or apply the entire proposition. The advantage of deductive development is clarity. Its disadvantage is the potential loss of tension or interest. The preacher must then work to rebuild the tension so that the remainder of the sermon validates or applies the entire proposition.

Discussing these various steps without an example is like handing someone the keys and saying, "Here, drive to the other side of Mexico City." The following draft of a sermon introduction will help you to see the logical flow. In brackets, within the text of the introduction, is my analysis of what I'm trying to accomplish.

> This week, with great honesty, one of you said to me, "Pastor Keith, if we hear one more sermon on suffering, I'm going to consider myself as "suffering" right there in church [give immediate relationship to this audience; see chap. 9 for the illustration hierarchy]. With truly pastoral compassion and sensitivity I responded, "Yes, but our study of 1 Peter has one more chapter, and we have to see it to see how to gain relief from our suffering." The person then began apologizing profusely. "I didn't mean to offend you. We all love your preaching, but . . ." Now with that comment, *I* began to suffer, from a little bit of my own pride.
>
> At first, I must admit, I felt a little stab. To suggest that our messages on suffering were themselves experiences of suffering did not exactly boost my ego. But I did not need to swing the pendulum the other direction, to be patted on the back [show personal relevance and how I've struggled with the issue of this sermon].
>
> We get "puffed up" about the silliest things, pastors not excluded. Ironic as it may sound, humility may unlock the door to relief from suffering.
>
> We all know people who have brought suffering upon themselves because of stubborn pride. But what does other suffering have to do with pride? We may think: "Well, when you're suffering, who's proud? If I'm suffering, I want to be built up, not humbled."
>
> One of my favorite children's stories is the one about the lion who gets a thorn in his foot. He hobbles around the jungle trying to find an animal brave enough to pull out the thorn.

All the time, he either overlooks a little mouse who is nearby, or in my interpretation, the king of the jungle won't humble himself enough to ask the mouse's help. Finally, as you come to the end of the book, the lion is exasperated. The little mouse volunteers to remove the thorn. The king of the jungle strikes a doubtful expression, but the mouse pulls and tugs and pulls and tugs and removes the thorn. Ah, relief at last! [introduce the thorn and paw as a concrete image].

In his instruction on suffering, which we've been studying in recent weeks, Peter said, "Humility may be just the thing you need to get some relief" [return to the context of the series in 1 Peter on suffering].

Now, what does Peter know that we don't? [begin to create an appetite for the text].

He knows that relief comes from the grace of a care-giving God [give a sneak peak at the point].

But he also knows that God's grace is stifled by human pride [probe what's at stake, and further whet the appetite for the text].

Now, here's what is significant about this relationship between pride and humility and suffering and relief:

When you know what God thinks about pride, God can begin to remove the thorn of suffering [first statement of the theological proposition; see chap. 4].

That's what we're going to see Peter saying to us about this strange relationship. He'll tell us how to remove the thorn to gain relief from suffering.

So, if you will suffer through one more message on suffering, we'll find the answer. We'll find it in three relationships that require humility: First, we must humble ourselves before the Lord. Second, we need humility in our relationships with other people. And third, we'll see that a humble trust in God to receive His care is essential, especially if we're ever going to get relief from suffering [preview the main structure of the message].

You recall that Peter was writing to people who were suffering at the hands of persecutors. They were suffering for their faith. We'd like to think that such things stopped in the first century, but all of you know about last week's tragic murder of a young evangelist on the university campus [give the context of the passage].

So, how do you remove the thorn to gain relief from suffering? Let's find the answer in 1 Peter 5. If you have a Bible, please turn to 1 Peter 5 and follow along as I read, beginning at verse 5. How do we remove the thorn of suffering? [create an appetite for the text and the sermon; establish a focus question that the text and the sermon will answer; orient to the text].

At my rate of speech, it takes just over five minutes to deliver the above introduction. Others will speak at a much different rate; some slower, some faster. The time invested in the sermon's introduction to demonstrate the relevance of the sermon to come is time well spent. It's worth the investment if, when we turn to the text of God's Word, we're all "on the same page," knowing why we should listen, what's at stake in the sermon for us, and what God has to say about this subject.

A second example should be helpful. We return to 1 Kings 18.

When I had the privilege of serving a church in southeastern Michigan as their pastor, a railroad track ran along the west border of the church's property. The track was used frequently, and it wasn't unusual for us to hear trains in the middle of services or at other times. The railroad crossing for the road that ran on the south edge of our property at that time did not have lights and guards that would come down when a train was passing through that intersection. There was only a stop sign.

One Sunday evening when the last few of us who were in the building were getting ready to leave, we heard sirens that obviously meant something was going on with emergency vehicles. Our youth pastor came running to me and said, "There's been an accident at the railroad crossing." He said,

"It's not anybody from church, but it's a young girl, and she's in pretty bad shape." A number of us walked out to the scene of the accident.

When I got to her car, it was very obvious to me that she was hurt severely; in fact she had nearly been decapitated, and the first thing I heard was the paramedic in charge telling one of the others to radio for the Life Flight helicopter. Not more than three or four seconds later he said, "No, cancel the Life Flight. We're not going to need it," meaning that the girl was not going to make it. Here was a sixteen-year-old girl, in the prime of life, on her way home from a family birthday party. She had not been drinking or anything of that nature and, somehow, even though she had been through that inter-section a number of times, failed to see or hear the train. She pulled out in front of it and tragically met her death.

Standing right behind me at the scene of the accident was a young man of, I suppose, college-age who had visited our church on a couple of occasions. I really didn't know him very well. We had been introduced and that was about all. As I turned around to walk back toward the building, he said to me, "Well, Pastor, where is she now?" I realized the arrogant tone with which he intended his question, and I kind of shrugged my shoulders and said, "Well, I'm glad I don't have to make that judgment call, but, like anyone else, I can say wherever she is depends on the object of her faith; had she trusted in Jesus as Savior or had she not?"

And the young man said, "Well, why would God let some-thing like that happen? If He's really a good and loving God, why would she even have such an accident?" And I realized that he was taunting me a little bit, but at the same time I think he was genuine about his questions, and so I began to interact with him about the fact that we live in a fallen world and that the tragedies and things that happen in this world are not a result of God's doing or wrongdoing but a result of our own depravity and our fall from the way that God created this world.

So we talked through those arguments for a little while, and I think he really was beginning to think that they had some merit. But I realized the more we talked about it that he really was just using the occasion to belittle the Christian faith, to poke fun and to say, "You know, why even consider God? This girl's gone. She only lived sixteen years. Her family is going to be devastated," and all of those kinds of things, with which I could not argue. And I realized that to continue to talk with him was basically futile because he had a completely different perspective of life, what, philosophically, we often call a completely different worldview. He was not even willing to be theistic, that is, to consent that there is a God, let alone to be *Christian* theistic, to say that the Christian God is the true God, and that He is sovereign and right in what He ordains or allows [relate the illustration to the subject to raise the subject].

Now, most of us are appalled at that example and think, "My, what an arrogant kid, that he would take advantage of a situation such as that to point his finger and prove his point!" But, we also realize that he's not all that unique. Every day we see, read, or hear hundreds of messages from commercials, billboards, sitcoms, news reports, and conversations at the coffee pot that tell us that people have a very different "worldview," a very different perspective of life, than the perspective given to us by the One who created life.

And, if we are going to be honest with ourselves, we have to stop and ask, "Why is it that we are so confident that we have the truth?" If there really is an absolute truth, if there really is one God, why are we confident that that God is our God, the Christian God, the God of Israel, the God of Abraham, Isaac, Jacob, Moses, and Jesus? After all, there are well-meaning, intelligent people in this world who follow other so-called "gods." There are well-meaning, intelligent people in this world who have argued strongly that there is no such thing as God. So how do we know, and who are we to assert such confidence in our faith? Who are we to trust God as if there is no other

God? When people challenge our faith like that young man challenged mine the night of that accident, I'd love to be able to just say, "Lord, send fire from heaven. Show this man. Turn this car into a chariot," or something like that and just have this wondrous sign that no one could deny right before their eyes. But most of us know that the showdowns that we have in our lives do not come that easily [show what's at stake].

So how do we know? How do we really know that our God is *the* God, that He really is *the* Creator of the universe, that He is who He claims to be? [begin to develop the focus question]. Are there some holes in our belief system? Are there some holes in our theology that we just can't explain? I don't think we can explain everything to the depths of our theology. Even Scripture says that God's ways are so deep they are past finding out, past explaining. But can we really be confident that God is who He claims to be, that He is *the* God, the *one* and *only* God, and that's why He commands, "Thou shalt have no other gods before me"? Well, we're hardly the first generation to ask such questions. In fact, even some of God's most faithful servants have been challenged in their faith to turn and ask such questions themselves [bridge the subject to the text].

The prophet Elijah, who was a bold proclaimer of God's message and plan, faced one of the biggest showdowns that any believer has ever faced in a place we today call Mount Carmel. In the ancient Near East where Elijah lived and ministered among people who thought much like the person at that accident that night, there were many gods that people talked about and worshiped. Many of these "gods" were idols created by the people. It's so perplexing that the people would worship a god that they made rather than the God who made them. But there were all kinds of gods, and so the people who said there was only one God, the God of Israel, were mocked. "How can you claim that your God is the true God? Why, it's ridiculous to pray to only one God and serve only one God. It would be a lot safer if you'd follow three or four different gods just in case you don't have the right one with your god." That was the prevalent thinking of the day. Kind of ruins the definition of God, though, doesn't it?

So, Elijah faced the followers of Baal with a very precise and vivid showdown to prove to himself and to those in the ancient Near East that there is only one true God. Through his experience we can know that our God, Elijah's God, is indeed the true God. We can know with certainty. We may not necessarily be able to convince others; it's not really our function to convince others. But we ourselves can know of God's sureness and His trustworthiness as the only true God. To come to that confidence, we need to see what Elijah was up against and understand the situation that Elijah faced and to witness how God proved Himself to Elijah and to the others [provide the context of the sermon's text].

In the Old Testament, the books of First and Second Kings provide a record of Israel's history from the beginning of the movement to place Solomon on David's throne through the end of the reign of Zedekiah, Judah's last king [provide the context of the sermon's text]. These books are so named First and Second Kings because they record and interpret the reigns of all the Kings of Israel and Judah, except Saul. Even David's last days are mentioned, though most of the events of his reign are recorded for us in Second Samuel and First Chronicles.

When Solomon came to the throne, Israel had no strong military threat among its neighbors. Both Egypt and Assyria were weak. Assyria grew stronger, however, and eventually attacked and took Samaria, the capital of the northern kingdom of Israel. Assyria attacked Judah some time later and, though it was able to take several southern cities, Jerusalem, the capital of the southern kingdom of Judah, did not fall. Assyria exerted control over Egypt, too, in 609 B.C. The pharaoh took his army north of Israel to Heron to assist Assyria in its threat from the neo-Babylonian empire. Thus, Assyria became a strong force and a strong threat to Israel.

So, when Elijah came to proclaim that the God of Israel

was the one and only true God, it's not surprising that others laughed and said, "Well, wait a minute. I think I'll go with the god of Assyria. I think I'll go with some of these other deities because they seem to have more going for them than your god does." And it is in this context that we find our popular story of Elijah's contest with the prophets of Baal. It's both an exciting and extremely significant account in the history of Israel. This whole period in which the kings reigned in Israel was a period in which God intended that the nation of Israel demonstrate to all people of the earth how glorious it can be to live under the government of God. How can we know that our God is the one and only true God? To answer that question we need to look together at Elijah's showdown on Mount Carmel. If you have your Bible, turn with me, please, to 1 Kings 18, and follow as I begin reading in verse seventeen [orient to the text].

In an introduction that provides this much context for the passage, we must be careful not to get sidetracked in a history lesson; nevertheless, some perspective of what Elijah was up against is critical to understanding the passage.

Conclusion

These nine elements of sermon introductions whet a listener's appetite for God's Word. When we move from the sermon's introduction to the body of the sermon, our listeners should know what we're talking about (the sermon's subject), know what's at stake for them (potential application), and want to hear God's Word address the subject.

YOU TRY IT!

Using the elements of relevant introductions described in this chapter, manuscript an introduction for a sermon based on Philippians 2:1–12. Before writing the introduction, you will, of course, need a grasp on the passage and to know the audience to whom you will preach. As with all sermon manuscripts, be sure to write for the *ear* rather than the eye.

4

Use Applicational Wording

The *general objective* in this chapter is to review and understand the three-fold process from exegesis to homiletics and thereby prepare the homiletical outline with people-focused applicational wording rather than text-focused exegetical wording.

The *specific objectives* in this chapter are

1. to understand the main moves on the road from exegesis to theology and from theology to homiletics;
2. to coordinate preparation tools (such as the Audience Relevance Worksheet) and presentation tools (such as the homiletical outline);
3. to see examples of people-focused wording for the sermon;
4. to connect application to the sermon's purpose.

The Expositional Process

Before going any further, we need to come to understand the expositional process, which leads to expository messages that are faithful to the text and that contain applications relevant to listeners. The expositional process is itself composed of three processes: exegesis, theology, and homiletics.[1] The moves through exegesis and theology to homiletics, up and down a ladder of abstraction, yield expository messages that do more than merely state theological principles. They yield messages that remain faithful to the text of Scripture while producing homiletical propositions with clear and relevant applicational imperatives.

The path from text to sermon is one that begins in the exegetical, travels through the theological, and reaches the homiletical. Although this overview of the expositional process comes as a sequence, the actual path from text to sermon is retroductive and includes a few U-turns to check and balance theology and exegesis. John R. W. Stott argues that preaching is a task that must work in two worlds—the world of the ancient text and the world of the modern listener. So the task of the preacher is to forge a path that leads to a bridge that spans the two worlds. Timothy S. Warren did yeoman's service by developing Stott's metaphor of the bridge and showing us how to cross it (via theology).[2] Warren's bridge will be discussed below in considering the theological process.

Process One: The Exegetical

The purpose of the exegetical process is to answer the question, "What does the text *mean?*" This is not simply asking, "What does the text *say?*" The distinction is between meaning and observation. In observation, the student of the Bible merely observes what the text *says*, without moving to *meaning*. One of the clearest examples of the difference between observation and meaning is found in dealing with figures of speech. Proverbs 18:10 reads, "The name of the Lord is a strong tower." Note the difference between observation and interpretation:

Observation: The sage declares that God's name is a strong tower.

Interpretation: The sage declares that God, in His character and attributes, is a place of security or refuge.

The exegetical process focuses on work with the text, beginning with a careful, critical reading in the preacher's native language. From this careful reading for initial understanding, the trained exegete then moves to the grammar, syntax, and lexical work in the original language as well as historical-contextual and literary study. *Exegesis focuses on the biblical audience (the original readers) and the meaning the text had for them. The exegetical conclusions (namely, about what the text means) will serve as the authority of the sermon.*

The result of the exegetical process is the exegetical product, stated as an exegetical proposition (similar to Robinson's "discovering the exegetical idea"). Two questions help the exegete synthesize the extensive analytical data required in exegesis:

1. What is the text talking about (narrowed subject)?
2. What is the text saying about what it is talking about (complement)?[3]

The exegetical proposition should include details about the text in somewhat pedantic language. The exegetical proposition or even exegetical outline includes the original time and audience. This is not a homiletical outline; thus, strict adherence to the *meaning* of the text is critical. When the preacher has a clear and confident grasp of the meaning of the text through exegetical conclusions, the second process begins.

Process Two: The Theological

The theological process is one that becomes more retroductive as the preacher now seeks not to "prove" that this is what the text means, but to demonstrate *what* this text may mean for any audience (neither the ancient nor the modern, but any audience). The result of the theological process is the theological product, stated as a theological proposition or a timeless principle. The theological proposition will not include the time-bound, pedantic language and details of the text, but rather will be worded for any audience. The theological process is critical in moving up the ladder of abstraction and crossing the *theological bridge* from the ancient world to the modern world. Figure 4.1 pictures this bridge.[4]

In the picture, the bridge between the two worlds is the theological process. The ladder at each end of the bridge is the ladder of abstraction. The preacher moves up the ladder at the left end of the bridge, from a specific exegetical proposition—or big idea—to a more general principle that applies to any audience, not just the original readers. Then at the right end of the bridge, the preacher moves down the ladder from general to specific, stepping into the homiletical phase, from the universal theological principle to the specific homiletical imperative for the preacher's audience.

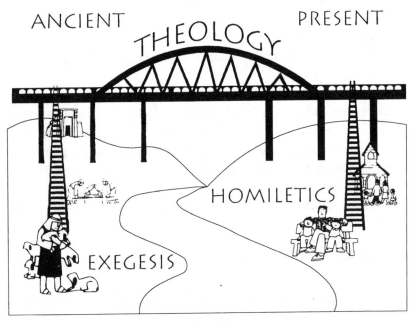

Figure 4.1

Process Three: The Homiletical

Suppose on our journey along the path from text to sermon we've carried a pair of binoculars. Peering through the theological lens opens the particular biblical theology so that it may be expressed in universal terms, or principles; the homiletical lens concentrates on the specific audience to whom the sermon will be preached. The specific applications, which carry the authority of exegesis and theology, will be different from one audience to another. Thus, the homiletical becomes "biblical truth applied." The homiletical proposition and perhaps even the homiletical outline will use applicational wording, usually in the imperative mood. Figure 4.2 summarizes the distinctions of the language of the three propositions or big ideas.

Exegetical	Theological	Homiletical
Biblical language	Timeless language	Contemporary language
Time bound to biblical author and audience	Covers all time and has no specific audience in view	Time bound to a specific contemporary preacher and audience
Technical wording	Nontechnical wording	Applicational wording
Information and meaning oriented	Perfection oriented	Application and motivation oriented
Provides analytical detail	Provides integrated truth	Provides interest and relevance
Textual order of the passage	Logical order of the argument	Communication order of a developed homiletical proposition
Concrete and specific	Abstract and general	
Declarative	Declarative	Imperative
Paul commanded the Philippian Christians to take on the attitude of Jesus so that they would serve one another.	Serving one another requires having the same attitude that Jesus had in coming to earth as an atoning sacrifice.	To be a servant, be like Jesus: Submit to God's plan.

Figure 4.2
Distinctions Between Exegetical, Theological, and Homiletical Propositions

Again, a brief example may help. The following figure compares and contrasts the Audience Relevance Worksheet introduced in chapter 2 and a homiletical outline (the "map" of the presentation) for Philippians 2:5–12.

Worksheet for Audience Relevance

When: Preparation in the homiletics phase

Purpose: To help the preacher think through what might for listeners function in the sermon as evidence

1. Conduct thorough audience analysis (theological, cultural, psychological, etc., as presented in chap. 1).
2. State the major claim being advanced.
   To be a servant, be like Jesus: Submit to God's plan.
3. Ask yourself, What might the audience demand as evidence to support the claim (biblical data, examples from life, personal illustrations, statistics, success stories, and so on)?
4. Ask yourself, What are the warrants, the connecting ideas between the claim and the evidence?
5. Ask yourself, Does the audience need qualifiers or reservations?

Potential Homiletical Outline

When: Preparation of the presentation (at the end of the homiletics phase)

Purpose: To prepare the order and relationships of what will be communicated

Homiletical
Proposition: To be a servant, be like Jesus: Submit to God's plan.

Purpose: Believers who hear this message will try to imitate the servant attitude of Jesus and submit to God's plan of service.

Introduction

1. Our mission statement says that we try to prepare godly servant-leaders.
2. Many of us are willing to be leaders, but servanthood doesn't come quite so easily.

3. Surely, we can learn how to be servants by looking to the example of one who is God, yet became a servant by coming to this world as a mere human.

4. How can we become godly servant-leaders?

[READ: Phil. 2:1–12]

I. Be like Jesus (v. 5).
   A. Do not try to *be* Jesus.
      1. He is God.
      2. You are not God.
   B. Do try to be *like* Jesus.
      1. Think like Jesus thought.
      2. Do what Jesus did by bringing people closer to God.

II. Be submissive to God's plan.
   A. Think about what is important (v. 6).
      1. Count your blessings because of who you are.
      2. Trust God and hold your blessings with an open hand.
   B. Think about how you can become the answer to others' problems (v. 7).
      1. Empty yourself.
      2. Serve others.
   C. Think about how low you must go to help somebody else (v. 8).
      1. Get down low (with all your Christian confidence).
      2. Obey God's plan to bring others closer to God.

III. Know that God will make it up to you.
   A. He will exalt you (vv. 10–11a).
      (Luke 14:11; James 4:10)
   B. He will be glorified through you (v. 11b).
      (Isa. 45:23; Matt. 5:16; Rev. 19:7)

Conclusion

1. Jesus is our supreme example of servanthood.
2. If we're going to imitate Him, we must be like Him in attitude and submit to God's plan.
3. To be a servant, be like Jesus, and submit to God's plan.

Often, preachers are tempted to stop with principles. Recently, I listened to a sermon that drove home the big idea, "Whether we live in crisis or contentment, God is always faithful and trustworthy." Though this theological principle gives a sound, biblical foundation to the sermon, I had to ask the preacher, "How did you want people to respond?" He replied without hesitation, "I want them to trust God regardless of their circumstances." I responded, "So why not tell them to do that?" Hence, the more homiletical/applicational big idea became: "Regardless of your circumstances, *trust God*, for He is always faithful and trustworthy." That may seem to split hairs or actually invite less audience participation than the principle that requires listeners to answer the *So what?* But many listeners need it spelled out in no uncertain terms. If the desired response is clear, state it boldly in applicational wording.

Connect Application to the Sermon's Purpose

At this point, with our exegesis complete, we have a pretty good idea about the meaning of the passage. And we know enough about the audience to begin thinking about our *purpose* for a specific audience. But how do we begin to develop the meaning of this passage into a sermon? When we think about developing a sermon, first we must think in terms of *purpose:*

- What am I trying to accomplish in this sermon?
- What does this audience need to hear?
- What was the biblical writer trying to accomplish?
- Should we be trying to accomplish the same thing?
- For what kind of applications does the text call?

It's not an overstatement to say that when it comes to preparing and delivering a sermon, purpose rules. The sermon's specific purpose (which is much more narrow than the overall purpose of preaching) gives precision to application. I find the categories used by social scientists helpful in specifying purpose and application. Social scientists research and instruct in terms of beliefs, attitudes, values, and behaviors (BAVB). Thus, at the top of every sermon manuscript, I write a purpose statement that becomes the compass for the entire sermon. While focusing on some aspect of BAVB, I find it helpful to write the purpose statement in terms of the *desired response,* rather than the preacher's aim. For example:

NOT: I purpose to persuade Christians to evaluate their financial giving practices to see whether they align with Jesus' teaching in the parables (preacher's goal).

BUT: Believers who hear this message will evaluate their financial giving practices to see whether they align with Jesus' teaching in the parables (desired audience response: behavior).

NOT: I want unbelievers to become Christians (preacher's aim).

BUT: Unbelievers who hear this message will trust Christ as their personal Savior (desired audience response: belief).

Four Caveats

I must mention four caveats. First, it is true that stating the sermon's purpose in terms of specific desired application(s) of beliefs, attitudes, values, or behaviors helps me to concentrate and keep the sermon on the track that calls for the desired response, but it is not my (the preacher's) responsibility to bring about that desired response. That is the Holy Spirit's work. Nevertheless, stating the purpose in specific applications helps to keep me focused. When I keep the sermon's purpose (desired response) in view, I lessen the risk of calling for a change in values when the biblical text calls for a change in beliefs. I cringe when I hear sermons (some of my own!) that preach for twenty-five minutes toward an attitude change and then suddenly ask people to change their behavior about something in the last five minutes. No wonder people don't respond.

The second caveat is that every sermon does not purpose to change something. Sometimes we preach for affirmation. Sometimes people are doing the right things and we should commend them. Overall, preaching purposes to change lives for the glory of God, but each individual sermon may not necessarily purpose a change. (Incidentally, it's wise for a pastor to "catch them doing good" occasionally and commend their listeners' obedience.)

The third caveat relates to persuasion. Some persuasion theorists have argued convincingly that people are persuaded better when they participate in the message. In other words, if the listener has to "make the connection," the message is probably more persuasive than if the speaker simply says "Do this!" Hence, we may be inclined to think that an implied imperative is more persuasive than the explicitly stated imperative. The old, and I might add, simplistic example is this: Which is more persuasive, the person who runs in the room and yells, "Get out of the building!" or the person who runs in the room and yells, "Fire!"? The latter is only an implied imperative, but because the desired response is so obvious and because it gives a greater sense of rationale than the former, it seems more persuasive. When it comes to God's Word, however, many people need the application stated in no uncertain terms. Hence, the homiletical big idea becomes an imperative proposition that states the desired response, according to the sermon's purpose. Figure 4.3 shows the relationship between the

"Charm is deceitful, and beauty is vain,
but a woman who fears the Lᴏʀᴅ is to be praised."
—Proverbs 31:30 (ɴʀsᴠ)

Intent of the text	Purpose Statement	Homiletical Proposition	Application
King Lemuel desired that women (and perhaps men) would seek their praise or admiration in their character (of fearing the Lord) rather than in outward beauty.	*Purpose:* That believers will develop a genuine fear of the Lord and thus be admired for their character.	If you want to be admired or appreciated, develop a genuine fear of the Lord.	To develop a fear of the Lord 1. regularly read God's Word. 2. praise more than you petition. 3. fear God's judgment more than you fear what people think.

Figure 4.3
Purpose-Proposition-Application Grid

sermon's purpose, big idea, or homiletical proposition and the application in regard to a message on Proverbs 31:30.

Notice the continuity between the text, sermon's purpose, homiletical proposition, and application. The continuity should keep the sermon on one track and lead to applicational wording that carries the authority of the passage.

The fourth caveat relates to behavior. Many times, we want to preach for behavioral response because behavior is much more observable than beliefs, attitudes, or values. Granted, there is a close connection between the latter three and behavior, but the change in belief, attitude, or values is no guarantee of a change in behavior. Hence, as you write the purpose statement, think carefully about the desired response or application. Review the questions on page 68. Be sure to preach for the proper response. With a clear purpose in view, you'll aim at the right destination.

Avoid Hypothetical Language

Another way to move to more applicational wording is to speak in the *real* instead of the *ideal*. Some preachers preach (and pray!) like they don't really believe what they're saying is possible. Either they speak in the subjunctive mood (a verb mood for the hypothetical) or they talk about "if" instead of "when." Consider the greater force in the preacher's statements when the subjunctive mood is changed or when we move from the *ideal* to the *real*.

Examples:

NOT: It is the desire of our hearts that we would be holy; or, We would be holy.

BUT: It is the desire of our hearts to be holy; or, We want to be holy.

NOT: If you want to be secure, trust God if you face overwhelming odds.

BUT: If you want to be secure, trust God when you face overwhelming odds.

Conclusion

Many listeners need the sermon's application pronounced in no uncertain terms, so state the desired application clearly and boldly. Everything in the homiletical phase of your sermon *must* grow out of sound exegesis and theology. The text *is* the authority for the sermon. We should not shy away from preaching the commands because through a process of exposition we make *thus says the Lord* relevant for our listeners.

YOU TRY IT!

You're to preach on James 1:2–11 in your church. You know the audience through analysis, or relationships, or both. Having already developed the exegetical and theological outlines, develop a first draft of a homiletical outline for the message. Be sure to use applicational wording for the homiletical outline.

5

Bundle a Packaged Deal

The *general objective* in this chapter is to see the necessity for unity in speech or public communication, and to delineate four tools to unify a sermon.

The *specific objectives* in this chapter are

1. to see why most listeners understand the message better when a sermon has unity;
2. to understand the strategies and see examples of using concrete images, closing the loop on an illustration, employing review/preview transitions, and sticking to the sermon's purpose.

Like computer technology, messages are easier to sell as packaged deals. Both Grady Davis and Haddon Robinson argue that an expository message should have one "big idea," thesis, or homiletical proposition.[1] Messages gain unity, however, through more than sticking to a single thesis. And tools exist that help us to maintain that unity by presenting the message as a neat package. How we introduce and conclude the message, for example, plays a significant role in tying up the package with one ribbon. Transitions that review and preview maintain the flow of thought from move to move. This chapter will discuss the necessity of unity in public communication and then describe the tools for doing so, focusing especially on preaching according to the sermon's specific purpose.

Duane Litfin summarizes the necessity of unity in speech or public communication, of which preaching is probably the most common example.

> There exists a remarkable consensus among those who have studied and practiced public speaking over the last twenty-five hundred years that the most effective way to structure a speech is to build it around a single significant thought. From the ancient Greek and Roman rhetoricians to the latest communication theorists, from the preaching in the Bible to the sermons heard in pulpits today, from the political oratory of democracies long past to the persuasive messages of our own times, the history of public speaking and the lessons we have learned from that history unite to argue forcefully that a speech, *to be maximally effective, ought to attempt to develop more or less fully only one major proposition.*
>
> The reason for this consensus stems from the way God has designed our minds. The human mind craves *unity.* Conversely, the thing we find most difficult to tolerate is chaos or randomness. For example, we look into the heavens and see a seemingly random mass of stars. But we are uncomfortable with such disorder, so we seek to discover patterns or "constellations." We try to organize what we see into a unity or a series of unities. Or again, we observe the phenomena of nature, including human nature, and find them on the surface to be complex and unrelated. Unhappy with this, we immediately begin looking deeper to construct a theory or hypothesis that will organize what we see into some sort of unified whole. This is the process we call "science." Or again, we consider the seemingly chaotic, unrelated details of the Kennedy and Martin Luther King assassinations. Such randomness is inherently dissatisfying, so there exists a natural

tendency to arrange the events into some unifying pattern or "conspiracy." This is as it always has been. The human mind is constantly seeking to discover unity in the stimuli it receives, to separate those items that seem to be related to one thing from those that are related to another.[2]

As we reflect upon the workings of the human mind, we soon discover why communication theorists hold to the value of the single proposition or big idea. As Litfin argued, the human mind has a God-given desire for unity, order, and progress. In the same way, the minds of those who listen to our sermons search for some overall unity.

If unity or order is the desire in communication, then how do we unify our sermons, that is, how do we bundle the sermon as a packaged deal? The remainder of this chapter describes four accepted strategies of public communication (or speech) that unify the sermon's message.[3]

Repeat a Concrete Image

As I argued in chapter 3, a single, concrete image repeated throughout the sermon, if not overused, has the power to unify, clarify, and give precision to the sermon. (See chap. 3 for an example of this strategy.) Because I have already given extended attention to this strategy, I will not repeat it here, but I will simply add that repetition of a concrete image is one of the strongest strategies for unifying a sermon. The power of metaphor is the power to hold and the power to hold together.[4] If an extended, repeated image is not possible, a valid alternative is the reprisal of an illustration.

Close the Loop on an Illustration

Strategic communicators often start a sermon with an illustration that provides promise for the sermon's application.[5] To build and maintain suspense in the sermon, the speaker does not conclude the opening illustration, however, thus tapping into our craving for unity or closure. In the sermon's conclusion, the speaker doubles back to the opening illustration to close the loop. Hence, the preacher ties a ribbon around the bundle; it becomes one package. One potential disadvantage of this strategy is that the reprise of the illustration signals the conclusion of the sermon and may therefore invite listeners to stop listening. If woven into the conclusion naturally, however, the speaker should actually increase attention by returning to the story for which listeners still want a resolution.[6] For example:

> That man with the loose tongue, what ever happened to him?
> No one has heard from him since.

Even if the illustration from the introduction was not left open-ended, simply mentioning the opening illustration again in the conclusion brings unity and closure.

But in addition to capturing our listeners' attention at the sermon's introduction and conclusion, we need to make sure that listeners travel with us throughout the sermon. For this journey, transitions that function as road markers are essential.

Employ Review/Preview Transitions

Transitions between the introduction and the body of the message, between the body and the conclusion, but especially between the main moves of the body of the message work well to communicate clearly and to help listeners follow us as we speak. Spoken words have no chapter headings, sub-headings, or paragraph indentations, so we must supply those in oral form.

Like the airport bus driver, if we inform our listeners where we're going, in what order, and how soon, they'll relax and enjoy the ride. If I board the bus at a strange airport knowing that I'm going to the Courtyard Hotel, I may get anxious when the driver pulls into the lot for the Hyatt; that is, unless as we boarded the bus the driver previewed where we'd be going. He or she could have simply said, "Okay, everyone, this is the bus for the Hyatt, Bellview, and Courtyard Hotels. We'll travel to the hotels in that order: first the Hyatt, then the Bellview, then the Courtyard." The clear preview of the route informs me that

I can relax because I'm going to be last to get off the bus. Without the preview, I wonder, *Why are we going into the Hyatt? Did I get on the wrong bus?* Then later I wonder, *Why are we going into the Bellview? I bet I took the wrong bus!* But because, as we leave the Hyatt, the driver says, "Now, from the Hyatt we'll go to the Bellview and then the Courtyard," I know that I'm on the right bus and still going to my destination. The driver simply supplied a *review* and *preview.*[7]

Similarly, the preacher who communicates (before moving into the body of the sermon) where the sermon will go and in what order ensures clarity and a smooth flow of ideas The preacher may simply preview the macro structure of the message by saying,

> This morning, in considering this matter of our words, we're going to see what God's Word says to us about the problem with our words, then the solution to the problem, and then the proper application of the solution.

Likewise, after the first major move, the preacher *reviews* and *previews* the structure of the message by adding,

> So, that's our problem. The tongue, our speech, has the ability to do great harm or great profit to others. Well, if that's the problem, what's God's solution to the problem?

This review/preview transition reminds the listener where we are in the big picture, just in case the listener is still back in the middle of the problem, thinking about that excellent illustration. You know, the story about the slandering man? Review/preview transitions orient listeners to the whole of the message, thus unifying the parts into the whole. Transitions, illustrations, and images, like everything else in the sermon, must submit to the sermon's purpose.

Stick to Your Purpose

While the overall purpose of preaching is to bring glory to God through the glad submission of the human heart (changed lives),[8] every

sermon has its own specific purpose that grows from the purpose of
the biblical text and the needs of the specific audience. I find it valuable
to write a purpose statement at the top of every sermon manuscript.
Like a road map, the purpose keeps me on the right road. As indicated
in chapter four, we write purpose statements in terms of the desired
audience response rather than the preacher's purpose. In addition to
the applicational purpose of a specific sermon, give attention to the
overall purpose of a sermon within the ongoing preaching calendar.

Bundle the Bigger Package

Another important way to bundle a packaged deal is to shape a sermon series by keeping in mind a sense of topical relevance. Even when
preaching an expository series through a book of the Bible, speakers
should help listeners grasp the topical approach to that series. Unfortunately, today's church attendance is not usually conducive to ap-
preciating consistency sermon-to-sermon, week-to-week. Hence,
every sermon needs to stand on its own, even in a series. All exposition is not necessarily exposition that moves sequentially through a
book of the Bible. But when we want to move through a book of the
Bible, often the study of that particular book (which will be very important to the preacher as we prepare the messages) is not nearly so
connected for our listeners. In other words, I may not be so concerned
that people know the outline of the epistle of James. I may be very
concerned, however, that they understand and apply James' messages
about the maturing of their faith. Pastor Chip Ingram of Santa Cruz
Bible Church and *Living on the Edge* radio ministry practices well the
strategy of bundling a sermon series. One of his short series progressed
as follows:

Series Title:	"Unquenchable Joy: Living Above Your Cir-cumstances"
Message One:	"Understanding the Power of Focus" (Phil. 1:1–11)
Message Two:	"Understanding the Power of Purpose" (Phil. 1:12–18a)
Message Three:	"Understanding the Power of Hope" (Phil. 1:18b–26)

Message Four: "Understanding the Power of Expectations"
(Phil. 1:27–30)

You'll notice that the above example is only a four-part series that serves as an exposition of Philippians 1. Listeners may not have heard or read the actual words "Series on Philippians 1," but they received the series title, "Unquenchable Joy: Living Above Your Circumstances," as well as the message titles on the power of focus, purpose, hope, and expectations, which for the listener fleshes out the intent of the series. In bundling the series package this way, Pastor Ingram, with relevant message titles, shows the messages' significance for his listeners and at the same time remains committed to the text of Scripture and the sequential exposition of God's Word.[9]

Conclusion

As our minds seek unity and God's Word comes to us in specific ideas or propositions, even in such genre as story or prophecy, bundled sermons—whether singly or as a series—are more readily received as a packaged deal.[10] Concrete images, closing the loop on an illustration, using review/preview transitions, and sticking to the sermon's purpose all help to bundle the bigger package and help our listeners to connect the dots.

YOU TRY IT!

Using the homiletical outline that you developed for chapter 4 (on James 1:2–11), incorporate review/preview transitions, a concrete image that will embody the big idea, and an overall "package" in the message's flow.

Unite People, Purpose, and Proposition

The *general objective* in this chapter is to show the value of uniting our understanding of the audience, our study of the biblical text, and our single proposition for developing the sermon.

The *specific objectives* in this chapter are

1. to understand how to develop the sermon so that it accurately "re-presents" the text for a specific audience;
2. to understand how each element—people, purpose, and proposition—informs the sermon's development, and how to bring them together for the sermon's development.

When people, purpose, and proposition meet, you're ready to develop your idea or proposition into a sermon. "People" provides the audience—you know the people to whom you will be talking (see chap. 1). "Purpose" gives specific direction for application or desired response—you know what you want to see happen (see chap. 5). The "Proposition," or big idea, unifies the sermon into a single statement that accurately re-presents the meaning of the biblical text with an eye toward application for your specific audience.

The question becomes, "How do the three elements work together?" A relevant biblical sermon requires all three elements. If "people" only drives the sermon, you'll be very relevant but not biblical. If "purpose" only drives the sermon, you'll be very applicational but not very instructive. If "proposition" only drives the sermon, you'll be clear and biblical, but you'll have little relevance. So we must work through the process of bringing the three elements together, which—following our exegetical and theological work from chapter 4—requires two *primary* steps.

Step One: Answer the Developmental Questions Related to Your Audience

We begin with Robinson's developmental questions. Notice that these are called *developmental* questions because they help us to *develop* the sermon.[1] Figure 6.1 breaks down the three developmental questions into sub-questions to ask yourself about your audience.

What does that mean?	Is that really true? (Do they "buy" it?)	What difference does that make? (So what?)
What did the author explain that my audience understands?	What did the author prove that my audience already accepts?	How did the author practically apply the proposition?
What did the author assume his audience would understand?	What did the author assume his audience believed?	How will I need to practically apply the proposition?
What will I need to explain to my audience?	What will I have to validate (prove) for my audience?	Where does the big idea show up in real life?
What can I assume my audience will already understand?	What can I assume my audience will already accept?	What changes or affirmations does this idea demand (in beliefs, attitudes, values, or behaviors)?
	What will it take to validate the big idea for this audience?	How can I concretely visualize this idea for my audience?

Figure 6.1

What does that mean?	Is that really true? (Do they "buy" it?)	What difference does that make? (So what?)
	What competing ideas need to be refuted briefly?	How can I help my audience feel this idea?

Figure 6.1 (cont.)

Using my church, in figure 6.2 I'll answer these questions for the sermon from 1 Kings 18.

What does that mean?	Is that really true? (Do they "buy" it?)	What difference does that make? (So what?)
What did the author explain that my audience already understands?	What did the author prove that my audience already accepts?	How did the author practically apply the proposition?
		The people worshiped God immediately
What did the author assume his audience would understand?	What did the author assume his audience believed?	
Baal worship	*That they could waver in their faith*	How will I need to practically apply the proposition?
What will I need to explain to my audience?		*Visualize situations in which we are tempted to waver and must believe that our God is the only true God*
A brief account of religious pluralism in the Ancient Near East	What will need validating (prove) for my audience?	
	That God is still the only true God even though we don't see Him send fire from heaven	
What can I assume my audience will already understand?		Where does the big idea show up in real life?
Challenges to God	What can I assume my audience will already accept?	*Every time we face temptation and must choose between obedience or sin; when people challenge us to be religious pluralists for the sake of tolerance*
	That Elijah represents God	
	What will it take to validate the big idea for this audience?	
	A brief apology (defense) for God's Word related to personal experience	What changes or affirmations does this idea demand?
		Unequivocal trust in God

Figure 6.2

What does that mean?	Is that really true? (Do they "buy" it?)	What difference does that make? (So what?)
	What competing ideas need to be refuted? *All religions are really the same; all these gods are the same thing*	How can I concretely visualize this idea for my audience? *Describe how the change in our lives brought by Jesus Christ's work is even more powerful than the fire on Elijah's altar; we are visual testimonies of God's power* How can I make my audience feel this idea? *Ask them about the wavering in their own hearts; ask them to recall times in their lives when God's work was so real that it seemed as if God had sent fire from heaven*

Figure 6.2 (cont.)

Step Two: Decide Which Developmental Question Will Dominate in the Sermon

As I answer the questions above, I see promise in and needs for application and validation. Some explaining will be necessary, but explanation will not drive this sermon. Thus, before I begin to structure the sermon with applicational wording (see chap. 4), I have to consider these three elements:

People: My church; I know them well. I know that they're challenged regularly by religious pluralism in schools, in the workplace, and at home.

Purpose: That listeners will believe that the God of Israel, the God of Abraham, Isaac, Jacob, and Jesus is the only true God.

Proposition: Trust God alone, for He is the one and only true God.

My introduction will probably begin with some question about trusting God or with the subject of religious pluralism. The structure of the sermon will develop the account on Mount Carmel, keeping the tension of the narrative and letting God's miraculous fire from heaven speak for itself. I like to develop narrative sermons around the canons of plot (exposition, conflict, complication, climax, and denouement).[2] I dare not, however, get lost in descriptions of the ancient Near East. So I must often remind the listeners that the issue of this sermon is our trust in God. After all, if Elijah's God is just one choice among many gods of equal standing, how can He be God at all, and why would He be trustworthy?

Again, a brief example may be helpful. After the introduction, the body of this sermon will probably develop something like this.

I. *Exposition:* To understand this account, we must understand a little about Baal worship, idolatry in Israel, and the leadership of Ahab and Jezebel.
II. *Conflict:* Elijah challenges the people to waver no longer but to choose God or Baal (v. 21).
III. *Complication:* Things get tougher as the account includes prayers and efforts of priests of Baal, Elijah's taunting, Elijah's preparations to demonstrate God's power (soaking the altar), and Elijah's prayer (vv. 25–37).
IV. *Climax:* When God burns the altar, the climax to the account is very vivid: Elijah's God is the one and only true God (vv. 38–39).
V. *Denouement:* The people cannot waver any longer. They must worship God alone. Like them, we must worship God alone. (v. 40).

I develop the sermon around the canons of plot to keep the tension of the narrative. The sermon itself will then have a bit of denouement, as I conclude with the homiletical proposition and its appropriate application for my audience. This focus works well to fulfill the needs for validation and application.

Conclusion

Too often, preachers develop their messages omitting one of the three elements: people, purpose, or proposition. Only when the three elements unite, however, can we be sure that we are re-presenting the text accurately and with proper precision in purpose and application.

YOU TRY IT!

You are to preach on James 1:2–11 at your church. Either through relationships or audience analysis, you know the people.

1. Answer the questions from figure 6.1.
2. Which developmental question will need most attention in this sermon and why?
3. Revise the homiletical outline you wrote for James 1:2–11 (chap. 4). Be sure to incorporate all three elements—people, purpose, and proposition—in your revision.

7

Adjust the Questions

The *general objective* in this chapter is to understand the value of adjusting the questions of listeners so that they will *want* to hear the sermon that answers a relevant question.

The *specific objectives* in this chapter are

1. to learn how to help listeners think along the lines of the sermon;
2. to learn (from seeing specific examples) the strategy of adjusting people's questions and thoughts to the question(s) that the sermon will address.

Relevant biblical preaching speaks to people's needs, but people are not always aware of their most significant needs. One popular approach to this dilemma is to tailor the preaching to "felt needs." This means, of course, that messages will speak to the needs of which people are aware. Unfortunately, people come to church with a wide variety of needs and questions. Many simply want an answer to the question, "What will get me through another week?" Many other people enter the gates of worship with even less significant questions on their minds: Where are we going to eat after church? Does Jimmy still need school clothes?

Even if the questions concern significant issues of the spiritual life, they are not necessarily the most significant questions that people need answered. If we preach only to "felt needs," our preaching will become dumbed down to address only popular topics rather than speak to the longings of the soul. But the experienced preacher knows that, as the message begins, many people are not asking questions that have to do with the longings of the soul. Hence, we need to adjust the questions.

Rhetorician Donald C. Bryant argues that the function of rhetoric is the function of "adjusting ideas to people and people to ideas."[1] In regard to expository preaching and in light of our commitment to the biblical text, rhetoric's function is limited to "adjusting people to ideas." Thus, we need to help people ask the questions that the sermon will answer. When I write about adjusting the people, I'm not thinking about manipulation. In fact, we must avoid manipulation. But adjusting people to the ideas of the Bible is part of the process of demonstrating the Bible's relevance. This process is similar to the format of the game show *Jeopardy!* In *Jeopardy!* an answer is given, and the contestant must respond with a question to fit the given answer. The preacher, just as in *Jeopardy*, must shape the focus question to fit the text's given answer. For example

> *James 1:2–4* = God uses trials in our lives to mature our faith.
> *Focus question* = Why does God allow those whom He loves
> to experience trials?

As another example, suppose I want my message to answer the question, "Is God your deepest longing?" That's not a question that people usually discuss around the coffee pot. So I might begin with something along these lines:

> What's your life really all about? What are you pursuing? Most
> of us are after something, whether it's the "American Dream,"
> a spouse, a higher paying job, a degree, or . . . you name it. Life
> is a pursuit.

I love the way that John Piper summarizes life's most important quest. He says, "God is most glorified in us when we are most satisfied in Him."[2] In what or in whom are you most satisfied? For many of us, the answer to that question is "my kids" or "my spouse." Or some of us who are willing to be honest might confess that we are most satisfied with the approval of our employer or our coworkers. A few of us might even say that we are most satisfied with a Cowboys win or Tom Hanks' latest film.

If we are Christians, however, it seems that Jesus Christ, our Savior and God, should hold our greatest satisfaction. If Dr. Piper is right that God is most glorified in us when we are most satisfied with Him, and I believe the Bible shows that Dr. Piper is right, we really need to ask ourselves, "Is God the ultimate source of my satisfaction? Is God my biggest joy?" And if He's not, how can we possibly expect to worship Him or to bring Him glory? Is God your deepest longing?

These opening lines of a sermon introduction are not yet refined, but they introduce what's at stake in the message and help people to focus on the question of their ultimate source of satisfaction, *the question that the text/sermon will answer.* From this start, I need to focus the introduction into one central question that the text (and thus the message) will answer (see chap. 3). All along the way, I'm telling my listeners what questions to ask. I could approach the subject less directly by surfacing a few questions that people may be asking themselves and then moving to the question that I want to address. But either way I have to help listeners feel the need for the question(s) of this message.

Another example may help demonstrate how we might adjust people's questions from what they're asking to what the sermon will ask and answer. Again, the approach is rather direct as I talk about questions, but you'll see the "adjusting."

What's the most pressing question on your mind this morning? Perhaps it's where you're going to eat dinner after church. Or perhaps you're stewing over how you're going to pay for that fender bender you had last Thursday. Some of you have deeper questions on your mind: Is Jason going to keep dating this girl? Will Mike do well on his SAT? Are the kids really developing their own relationships with the Lord, or are they just conforming to the expectations of the Christian community?

These are interesting and important questions, but we wouldn't necessarily say that any one of them is life's most important question. What is life's most important question? This morning I want to suggest to you that life's most important question is, "What is the greatest desire of your life?" If you're single, it may be a life partner. If you're a vice-president, it may be a promotion to president. If you're a young married couple, it may be a child. There's nothing necessarily wrong with any of those desires, unless they take God's place as the ultimate desire of your heart.

I love the way that John Piper summarizes life's most important quest. He says, "God is most glorified in us when we are most satisfied in Him."[3] In what or in whom are you most satisfied? For many of us, the answer to that question is "my kids" or "my spouse." Or some of us who are willing to be honest might confess that we are most satisfied with the approval of our employer or our coworkers.

If we are Christians, however, it seems that Jesus Christ, our Savior and God, should hold our greatest satisfaction. If Dr. Piper is right that God is most glorified in us when we are most satisfied with Him, and I believe the Bible shows that Dr. Piper is right, we really need to ask ourselves, "Is God the ultimate source of my satisfaction? Is God my biggest joy?" And if He's not, how can we possibly expect to worship Him or to bring Him glory? Is God your deepest longing? What, or who, is your greatest longing? Is that question pressing for you today? *Is God your deepest longing?*

Here, the topic for the sermon example lends itself to talking about questions. Most topics will not explicitly talk about questions; the preacher will have to adjust the questions with more subtlety as shown in this next example.

> When I was in high school, and for a couple of summers between years in college, I worked in a large, old-time hardware store and lumberyard. It was the kind of store in which you could buy just one wood screw or one faucet washer if that's all you needed. And we prided ourselves in having the hard-to-find hardware. Employees had to work the whole store, and though we didn't have departments in the store, my favorite area was "security"—lights and locks. In fact, when the store needed a resident expert in security, I volunteered for some training on locks.
>
> Do you know what kind of door requires a double-sided deadbolt? Or do you know which deters prowlers better, lights or locks? See, it was fun to work in security: You could scare people into buying almost anything!
>
> Sadly, at times, I think people really thought that's what they were buying: security. What they really wanted was the absence of fear, no risks or danger. Yet, in this world, life is full of fears. Some fears are even good because they warn us about genuine dangers.
>
> Security is confusing in our world because we have so many varieties: home security, job security, financial security, marital security, social security, national security, and so on. But what is real security? By *security*, I don't mean happiness or even contentment. I mean the confidence to know that you can handle whatever comes your way. Perhaps the courage to hear your physician say, "You have a form of cancer." Or maybe even the security that you want to have when your spouse goes out of town for ten days. No lock or light can provide that kind of courage or security. *So, what is genuine security and how do we get it?*

These introductions will now go on to utilize the strategy of chapter 3: "Whet an Appetite for God's Word." But before we can move to the text for the sermon, we must have people thinking with us about how the message relates to them, showing them *what's at stake for them* in the sermon. We do that by bringing them to the question that the text and sermon will answer.

Complete the Subject

Shaping the question to the answer develops the sermon as a subject to be completed. Sermons take other shapes, however. For example, in *Biblical Preaching*, Haddon Robinson argues that sermons may take various shapes, including

- an idea to be explained
- a proposition to be proved
- a principle to be applied
- a story to be told
- a subject to be completed[4]

I agree with Robinson's possibilities. (I'm sure he's thankful.) For the sake of relevance, however, it seems that every sermon has to raise a significant question that the text will answer and that introduces the sermon's *subject*. If the introduction does not raise the sermon's subject, one is left to wonder what has been introduced. It could be contended that raising the question that introduces the subject will allow the sermon to take only an inductive approach. In induction, the preacher usually argues from specific concepts to a general conclusion (proposition or big idea). If the sermon is deductive—stating the big idea and then developing it with explanation, validation, or application—the "cat is already out of the bag" (so to speak); thus, the question has been answered before moving to the body of the sermon.

The preceding charge is accurate to some degree. The deductive sermon will lose tension, attention, and retention, *unless we give the listener something to anticipate further in the sermon.* Speech theorists have long argued that public speaking is the developing and answering of a question.[5] So the deductive sermon may not ask a question that introduces a subject to be completed, but it will raise a question that begs for an answer from God's Word. Again, an example should help. Here is an introduction for a deductive sermon.

> I know that most of you find it hard to believe that I could ever be "speechless," but last Sunday afternoon, it happened. The wife of one of my best friends called to say that her husband, a pastor in another state, had confessed to adultery and taken off with the other woman. I could hardly even say anything to her; I was so stunned. If you had asked me to make a list of the people that I thought would never fall morally, he would have been on that list. But he didn't make the team. How? Why? How does it happen that a guy who has a wonderful, and I might add, very attractive, wife, a beautiful family, growing ministry, and so much going for him, just throws it all away for a few moments of pleasure? Has he not counted the cost accurately? Is he lonely? Is he deceived? How does that happen?
>
> Apparently, this problem is not new. Way back in the Old Testament, the wise sage, Solomon, gave counsel to his son. And it's that counsel that I want us to take from here this morning. In a nutshell, Solomon told his son, *Avoid sexual sin by counting the cost.* That's the point that we all need to hear. So, naturally, we have to ask ourselves, "How do we count the cost?" We find clear directions for counting the cost of sexual sin in Proverbs chapter 5. Please turn in your Bible with me to Proverbs 5 so that we can see God's instructions for counting the cost to avoid sexual sin. How do you count the cost?

In the deductive sermon, the answer to the question will not complete the big idea (or provide the complement for the subject). That's already been done. The remainder of the sermon will have a very applicational, "how-to" approach that should both validate and apply (second and third developmental questions) the big idea.

Conclusion

Adjusting people to ideas, that is, adjusting people to biblical ideas, is part of the process of demonstrating the relevance of God's Word. We cannot assume that people are interested in the Bible, even if they ask questions related to spiritual formation. To show them the relevance of God's Word without changing the message of God's Word, we must adjust the people to our questions.

YOU TRY IT!

Back to your church and your sermon on James 1:2–11. Write the first draft of your introduction by adjusting the listeners' questions to the subject of the sermon. Reviewing chapter 3 may be helpful.

8

Tell 'n Show

The *general objective* in this chapter is to discern the value of "picturing" application for our listeners.

The *specific objectives* in this chapter are

1. to provide the promise of successful application for our listeners;
2. to help our listeners understand *how* to make application of biblical truth.

A mother was writing an excuse for her kindergartner, who had been home sick with a stomachache. As the child observed her writing, he said, "Okay, Mom, but don't say I threw up. I want to save that for 'Show and Tell.'"[1] In kindergarten we show and tell. In relevant biblical preaching, we tell and show. We *tell* the truth of God's Word and *show* people how it shows up in life. We need to preach every sermon as if we were talking to people from Missouri. They sit in the pew or chair and think *Show me.* This chapter offers several ways to "picture" application. We begin with the merits of picturing others' success in the application of biblical truth.

Show Success Stories

We mentioned successful application in chapters 2 and 3. When others succeed in applying the truth of God's Word, it helps us to think, *If she did that, I probably could, too.* Or we might think, *So that's what he means.* These examples of successful application are "success stories." By *success*, I mean success in obedience, faithfulness, believing what God's Word says, and doing what God's Word says to do. It's not enough to tell people that our trials come with God's purpose in view. God wants to strengthen our faith. That message is clear in James 1. But many of us wonder, as we go through the trial, "Is this really okay with God? Is He really strengthening me?" If we do not believe what James 1 tells us about the purpose of our trials, we will not follow the command to "consider it pure joy . . . whenever you face trials of many kinds" (James 1:2). So a success story of someone actually doing that adds credibility to the notion that we could do that, too.

> As many of you know, my mother died from breast cancer just as I was beginning my sophomore year of college. The summer before she died, I often spent the evenings sitting with my mom. Some nights, she was so "out of it" that all I could do was sit there to hold her hand. Other nights, she had "lecture notes" written for me. Her primary lecture that summer was "How to Find a Wife and How to Treat Her Once You've Found Her." I listened very attentively. I recall one evening about six or seven weeks before she died, when my mom just paused in the middle of her "talk" to say, "You know, if I were not this sick, in this hospital, we may never have had this talk. I'm not glad for cancer, but I'm glad for this time." She could consider it joy.
>
> More than that, my mom, who was a nurse, developed a very close relationship with a Christian nurse who had had cancer herself. And Mom led two of her nurses to the Lord. My faith grew a lot that summer as I learned to trust that God knew what we needed more than we did. Mom was right. It really was joy.

The above story comes out of the pages of my life and the page of a sermon manuscript. We don't always have such apropos illustrations or those with so much tenderness, but if we know the people to whom we preach and we observe life, success stories abound. Chapter 9 gives some guidelines for illustrations, but one guideline deserves mentioning at this point. Whenever you use a success story as an applicational illustration, get permission from the person and tell others that he or she has given permission.

As will be seen in the illustration hierarchy in chapter 9, success stories that come from my own life or the lives of those in the audience carry the most potential to impact listeners. We have to be careful, though, with personal success stories, for we may be perceived as superhuman or holier than thou. Nevertheless, the closer the illustration is to the audience, the more potential for impact it has. Sometimes, however, our application needs to picture something short of success.

Show Failure Stories

We do not want to become "negative preachers." I once sat under the ministry of a negative preacher, and I wondered if he'd ever read the gospels. But just as we need to picture what good application looks like, occasionally we need to picture disobedience or failure. Obviously, we don't want to use someone from the audience, but we do need to picture the wrong kind of response, or the kind of response to avoid, and if possible use an example from real life. Here is a brief example.

> I attended a funeral service one day of a pretty wealthy man who had five sons, all of whom had been very successful in business endeavors. I thought before the pastor said "Amen," two of the brothers were going to come to blows. They entered the chapel "having words." Throughout the eulogy and service, they leaned over to each other to continue their argument. I have no idea what was at stake, but it was more important than Dad. When the service concluded, one of the

brothers stood up and stormed out, hitting his fist on the chapel door as he left. The other brother looked at him and shrugged his shoulders. At that, the youngest of the five stood up to scold the remaining brother. Before the casket was moved, the funeral director had to hold back the one brother from hitting the young brother. Had the funeral director not jumped in, it might have looked like a scene from a Western movie's barroom brawl. That's not what the writer of Ecclesiastes means when he says, "There is a time for everything." In fact, it may mean just the opposite. He may mean, "Do things at the proper time." Whatever the issue at that memorial service, surely it could have been settled later.

Tell the Story Well

Throughout this chapter, these strategies for showing application have in common the value of story. Story brings practice to principles, action to experiences. Stories beckon the senses. Commands and principles merely state the facts. But showing the application in story shows application in life. One guideline for applicational stories is necessary: Give enough detail to beckon the senses, but not so much that we wander into a separate sermon. Grant and Reed summarize:

> We often feel compelled to pack our stories with all the truth there is on a given subject. It's a fine sentiment, but we cannot afford to yield to the temptation to "cram." Yes, we want to be thorough in our study of the lesson, but as I have heard Howard Hendricks say in the classroom, "We don't want to dump the whole load of hay on one heifer!" You can't include all there is to know (or even all that is known) about justification, for instance, in one story. Give people truth in bite-size chunks that are easily digestible. Show them how God's truth works in life through a good story, and you may even get them into the Word for themselves![2]

The following example attempts to follow Grant and Reed's advice.

So, sometimes, we're planting or watering when we don't even know it. But God's Spirit is at work. One of my best friends in high school and I really had very little in common. He was a rich kid who got everything he ever wanted. He knew the value of nothing. He was not the wildest kid in school, but he got around. I was a young Christian, struggling like many Christian teens to be a Christian and a teenager at the same time. On a few occasions I talked with him about the Lord. He was kind enough to listen usually, but he made it clear that it wasn't for him. Maybe he didn't see anything in my life that he wanted. I don't know if my time with him had any value for planting or watering, but about a year ago, I learned that he has become a Christian and is walking closely with the Lord.

What I didn't mention in this short story is the beautiful sports car he drove, the fact that he had grown up going to a church that did not preach the gospel, or that he and I have had almost no contact since high school. These details are interesting, but unnecessary to make the point about planting and watering.

See It First Yourself

Before you can show something to someone else, you have to see it yourself. That's especially true for the application of God's truth. To script the story as you want to tell it, you have to see the actors, the action, and the images that are going to take place in the story. One of my favorite stories is about a man who approaches an elderly couple who are eating in McDonald's. I can see McDonald's in my mind, and most people in North America can visualize their local McDonald's, what the tables are like, and what it looks like when somebody leaves the counter and carries his or her tray over to a table. So it's not very hard to share those images and communicate that story.

For the few people in your audience who have not been in a McDonald's, it may be more difficult to get across those images. You may have to describe the counter, the distance to the table, why they use trays, and some things along those lines, but you can still tell the story. But first you have to see it yourself. Once you can see it, you want to play the videotape of the story for your listeners. In playing the videotape, you write the script for the story, thinking again of the images and the action that you see in the story. What exactly do people themselves need to "see" in order to understand this story?

After you have the story scripted, be sure to test it on someone. That is, test your telling of the story to your spouse, a ministry colleague, or a friend, in order to find out if they see it as you see it. When telling the story, you may have to use a small amount of sermon context, or the point will not be as obvious as you desire. Tell the story and then ask your guinea pig, "What's the point of the story?" Then ask him or her to tell the story back to you. Even if your tester isn't a good storyteller, you'll pick up whether he or she pictured the same details that you pictured. Careful attention to this precision in the telling of the story is vital to proper application lest your listeners define your application through the eyes of their own experience rather than what you envision. What we're trying to do is create the experience for them and to help them see it as we see it.

Offer Variations

Some applications come in the form of visual suggestions. The value of these snippets is that the preacher can suggest variations of application, and thereby cast a broader net. It is imperative, though, that these variations do not come across as a list, but as experiences. Consider the following example.

> When it comes to loving one another, there's no single, concrete way to carry out this command. I think of Phil and Vivian. God has blessed them financially for many years. They've traveled the globe sharing their blessings with so many missionaries that even they lost count. Or I recall one time, in our first church, when one of our deacon's wives was home sick with three sick kids. My wife threw together a

delicious version of homemade cream of chicken noodle soup and took it over to their home for dinner. What a welcome she received! And do you know what the thank-you note said? "Your expression of *love* meant so much." I think all of us know that one of the best ways to love others is to listen to them. I have a friend who likes to stop by my office on his way home from work. He likes to vent. He doesn't come for advice. He doesn't seek counsel or wisdom (thankfully). He just wants to vent. So, I sit there and let him vent. It may sound like a strange form of Christian love, but he needs to vent, and so I listen. Loving one another can take many forms in our lives. Many of the forms are the little things that mean so much as we journey through life together.

In this example, I've cited three possible applications, but I've told them as three experiences, or three *real* stories. As people hear them as stories, they have much more emotional and volitional impact than if I simply said, "You could help someone financially, or take a meal to someone who's sick, or just listen to somebody." That's the difference between telling and showing. In preaching with relevance, we need to tell *and* show.

Conclusion

In kindergarten we show and tell. In relevant biblical preaching, we tell and show. We *tell* the truth of God's Word and *show* people how it shows up in life. Stories play a major role in our "showing." We need to show success stories, and perhaps a few failure stories. Showing rather than merely telling the application relates the biblical truth to experience and takes the truth out of the abstract and brings it to the concrete.

YOU TRY IT!

In your message, you've been talking about commitment. But how can we *see* commitment? We do not usually see commitment, but rather the results of commitment. "Show" us a success story of commitment from your own life or the life of someone in the audience. Write (for the ear) a paragraph that will *show* what you've told.

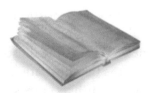

Illustrate According to Purpose

The *general objective* in this chapter is to understand the value of choosing illustrations according to purpose.

The *specific objectives* in this chapter are

1. to see and understand examples of three general purposes that illustrations usually attempt to accomplish;
2. to use the illustration hierarchy to provide close connection to our listeners;
3. to follow several guidelines for using illustrations effectively.

My wife often hears or reads an interesting story or comment and remarks to me, "There's a good illustration," or "I heard a good illustration today." Being a good wife, she knows that I beg, borrow, and steal illustrations for preaching. But she also knows that my pat reply is, "Illustration of what?" *To illustrate* is a transitive verb, meaning it demands an object. A definition of *illustration* might read as follows:

Any modus operandi by or through which eventuates the re-
ciprocal transposition of information between or among enti-
ties or groups via a commonly understood system of symbols,
signs, or behavioral patterns of activity, referent of another
object or stimulus, for the purpose of elucidation of the object
or stimulus.[1]

Said more simply, the story, the statistic, the quotation, or the startling statement is not illustrative until we attach it to an object. The
question, then, becomes, "What is the illustration designed to do?"
or, more precisely, "What is the illustration designed to illustrate?"
The illustration must accomplish its purpose or it's just a story, a statistic, or a sample, but it's not an illustration. It's not an illustration
without a connection to its object. The root meaning of the verb *to
illustrate* is "to shed light upon" or "to illumine." Thus, until our
story, statistic, sample, or data shed light on something, it fails to illustrate because there's no clear connection between it and the intended object.

An illustration is sometimes designed to accomplish more than one
purpose, but the essential purpose of an illustration falls into one of
three categories: explanation, validation, or application. You might
think, *What if I just want to give an example?* Giving an example is
not your purpose; it is your means. Your purpose would still be to
explain, validate, or apply, and sometimes an example can do any, or
all three, of those purposes. There may be other objectives in view,
but when you use an illustration, you're usually trying to explain,
validate, or apply.

Figure 9.1 shows the more specific purposes that fall under the three
larger categories. In his book, *The Art of Illustrating Sermons,* Ian
MacPherson listed seventeen purposes for sermon illustrations.[2] But
when examining McPerson's lists of purposes from a rhetorical stand-
point, it can be concluded that they fall under one of the above three
categories. In discussing each of these categories, this chapter uses
examples to show the differences as well as the overlap in these overall purposes. Guidelines for using illustrations will also be provided
and discussed.

Illustrations *purpose* to:

Explain Objective: understanding	Validate Objective: agreement	Apply Objective: obedience
Expand	Gain Agreement	Provide a "How To"
Clarify	Prove	Show the Significance
Elucidate	Show as Realistic	Make the Impact Felt
Simplify	Make Believable	Touch a Need
Specify	Convince	Relate Truth to Experience
		Show the Truth in Action

Figure 9.1

Illustrations to Explain

When you use an illustration to explain, you may want to expand, clarify, elucidate, simplify, specify, make something concrete, or contrast things, but your overall objective is to stimulate understanding. When we think about explaining something, we are tempted to think about lengthy, drawn-out illustrations, but some explanatory illustrations are quite brief.

Analogy: Integrity is to Christian leadership as egg is to omelette.

Concrete: It was a Russian-made car about the size of a Honda Civic.

Contrast: This isn't the kind of knowledge we have when we say, "I know someone at work." It's the kind of knowledge we have when we say, "I know my wife."

Figure: Where there's light, there's bugs.

Conversely, some illustrations that explain are rather lengthy, or may even require a story. Consider this example from Pastor Bill Hybels' preaching:

About ten years ago I decided to take up the sport of racquet-ball. Now, one game is all it took to get me hooked. I just loved the game from the first time I played it. I started play-ing it regularly and then I started playing it frequently and, after a while, I was playing it four to five times a week. In those days court time was cheap; I think it was about $4 an hour. So I'd invite a friend to come and play and split the cost. He'd pay $3. I'd pay $1. Being Dutch I'd arrange it that way. But in only a matter of months I was winning almost every single game I played. Of course, I was screening my oppo-nents very carefully, playing mostly the elderly, the infirm, and so on. But there was no question in my mind that I had found a sport that I could play really well. I caught on to that game fast.

Now, one day at the club where I played I saw a poster announcing that there was going to be a tournament at our club that month. And I was new to all this, didn't understand how they went, so I was reading the poster. The poster said the way it was set up is that there would be three skill levels. There would be the C level and that would be for recreational novices. Then there would be a B level and that would be for serious racquetball players. And then there was an A level, and I gathered from how they described it that these were the guys who slept with their racquets. But I remember standing there and looking at that poster and thinking to myself, "Now if I enter this, this being my very first tournament, I wonder what would be the appropriate skill level for me." And be-cause I was a Christian, you know, a minister, teacher of the Word of God, I knew all that the Bible said about humility, and so I said to myself, "Admit it, Bill, you're probably not an A-level player. You know you've only played a few months, you're probably not going to win the A level." The Bible says to think soberly about ourselves; you know, have sober judg-ment about yourself. So, I applied that to my situation. So I stood there and tried to figure out should I play it safe by entering the B level, or should I just throw caution to the wind and sign up for the A level and try to pull off an upset victory? One thing was for sure: I had no interest in the C league whatsoever. I was way past this recreational novice business.

Now, as I was finalizing my decision there to jump right into that A level an older gentleman walked up to me and he said, "Are you going to enter the tournament this month?" And I said, "Well, I'm thinking about it." And I could tell he was checking me over and sizing me up, trying to figure out how good I might be, maybe what class I was going to enter. And I was checking him over and wondering, trying to size him up too, wondering what class he might be in. And I was looking at a little potbelly guy, short guy, no reach. You know, in different sports you look for different things. Real short little arms on this guy. And, again, older guy, sort of looked like the family pharmacist, or someone like that. Am I going to get in trouble for saying that? I was going to say like a librarian but I thought we might have some so I didn't want to do that. I was pretty sure we didn't have any pharmacists. Well, maybe we did. Sorry about that. Well just . . . you get the idea of the kind of person I'm trying to describe. But, anyway, he said, "I entered last month's tournament." I said, "What league?" He said, "C." I thought, "Figures." And then he said, "And I came in 10th." It was like he was proud of it. And I thought to myself if I came in 10th place in the C league I wouldn't tell a soul. You know, it'd be embarrassing. Then, out of the blue, the guy said, "Well, you know, I've already played a couple of games this afternoon, but if you're looking for a game I'd be happy to play you." And I said, "Okay." You know, figuring that this would be kind of a benchmark game for me. I could gauge the level of play of a C guy and then I could enter the appropriate level of play for me, probably A or B. Now, to make a long story short, this potbelly, short-armed little guy beat me 21-zip in about seven minutes. [laughter.] Ah, come on, don't get ugly now. I mean, I'd never seen a racquetball hit that hard, go that fast, or hit that low. I felt I needed a spatula, not a racquet. Unbelievable. He *annihilated* me. We chatted after the game, back in the locker room. He didn't even have to shower. I only did because I was recuperating from a weeping spell that I just had. But I asked this sort of Carl Malden clone, you know, I said, "Could I ask you a few questions, just a couple of questions? Now, you said you placed 10th in the C league?" He said, "Yeah. You know, I had a good tournament." I said, "Now, if you were to have played the guy who won the C league last month, if you were to play him, what do you think the score would be?" He said, "Probably 21-5." He said, "I'd like to think I could get 5 points on him." I'm thinking, "This guy whipped me 21-zip and he's going to get beat 21-5 by the C-league winner?" I said, "Well. What would happen if an average B-level guy played the winner of the C league?" He said, "It'd be ugly. Murder. Slice and dice. 21-0." He said, "I'd guarantee that C-league winner wouldn't probably even get a point on a good B-league guy." I'm feeling weaker all the time. And I said, "Well, then what would happen if any A-league guy played a B-league guy?" He said, "Same thing. Slice and dice. It'd be over in a matter of minutes." I was real weak then. He said, "You ought to see what a pro does to an A-league guy." And then the old guy said, "Oops! I'm running late. I gotta go. Enjoyed the game." And I thought, "Bet you did."

So I sat there all alone in the locker room thinking to myself, How deceived can a person be? Twenty minutes ago I thought I was almost an A-league player. I might even win it. I was certainly a B-league player and in the hunt in the B league. I didn't even want to mess with the C level and then I just got clobbered by a guy who wound up in 10th place in the novice league. How deceived can a person be? I mean, let me state the obvious. I had vastly overrated my abilities. I had never objectified my skill level before I played him. I didn't have any benchmark by which to assess my level of play. And when I stumbled across this guy he became the kind of benchmark that made me face reality. I had overrated myself.

You know, athletics isn't the only arena where people overrate themselves. Sometimes it happens in the political arena.

A guy gets all enthused about running for a particular office, and he does the whole Kennedy routine, and he predicts he's gonna win by a landslide. Election day comes. He gets slam-dunked. He loses. He has himself overrated. Drexel, Burnham, Lambert in the financial field had themselves a bit overrated on Wall Street until reality struck with a vengeance recently. People can overrate themselves in the financial arena. But nowhere does the problem of overrating oneself happen more frequently than in the spiritual realm. And let me just come right out and say it. Most people vastly overrate how good they are in the eyes of God. Most people walk around believing that they're capable of competing at the A level of morality in God's sight. And, well, if they're not at the A level, they're going to place in the B level, you can bet that. Nobody sees themselves as being a C-level player along the lines of morality. Nobody.[3]

Here, Pastor Hybels gives us an extended illustration to make the point that people overestimate their morality. Notice that the illustration preceded the point and that he "debriefed" the illustration to make sure that his listeners got the point. He clarified that the point was not about racquetball, but about overestimating our morality (very similar to how we sometimes overestimate our athletic ability). What if he had simply started the sermon by saying, "Most people way over-estimate their morality?" That statement would obviously have had nowhere near the impact that the explanatory illustration provided. In his explanatory illustration we could see and feel the faulty premises of our judgments, the power of human pride, and the necessity of humility as we evaluate ourselves. So Pastor Hybels' illustration may have spilled over into the validation category. But he was, in essence, explaining how we overrate our spirituality.

Illustrations to Validate

When you use an illustration to validate, you may be trying to gain agreement, prove something, show it as realistic, make it believable, convince people, relate truth to tangible experiences, or weaken resistance. It does not follow logically that an example validates. But speaking rhetorically, examples often bring agreement in the "Oh, so that's what he means!" sense. Hence, as you validate you may weaken resistance or lessen the argument of those who are thinking, "Is it really like that?" The following example uses humor in an attempt to weaken resistance to the idea that our tendency to seek revenge is natural.

> Revenge seems so just. Forgiveness seems so inequitable, even impossible. The column in *Reader's Digest* explained that it was about midnight at one of those 24-hour truck stops. There was a husky, brawny truck driver sitting alone in a booth, getting ready to take his first bite from a massive double-cheeseburger. The door of the place swung open and in walked eight loud-mouthed members of a motorcycle gang. The only place big enough to seat all eight of them was the booth where the trucker was sitting. So one of the bikers marched over and told the trucker to get up and sit someplace else. Well, the truck driver looked around for another table but the place was packed and so he just reached down for his cheeseburger as to go about his business. Well, the biker was not going to be outdone so before the trucker could pick up the burger the biker grabbed it off the table and began eating it. When he finished he said, "Now, your meal's done. Get up." When this trucker stood up, he was about two heads taller than that biker and the look in his eye could have pierced iron. The trucker reached down to that table and he snatched up the check, walked over to the cashier, paid the bill and then calmly walked out the door. Well, the bikers began to laugh, and the guy who ate the burger walked over to the cashier, kind of glanced out the window and said, "Well, that fellow ain't much of a man is he?" "No," she said. "Doesn't appear to be much of a driver, either. Just ran over a whole row of motorcycles." Revenge seems so just.

By using humor, we try to weaken resistance or show that the subject is realistic or believable. You may wonder if the fictitious story of the trucker and the bikers can make something believable, but the illustration simply identified our human tendency toward revenge. The story made the emotion or tendency toward revenge become realistic. And the humor helped to break down our listeners' resistance because they could relate to the emotional tendency. Then when the sermon moves from the subject of revenge (a problem) to the complement of forgiveness (the solution), it is hoped that our listeners' reactions to what doesn't come naturally are sufficiently weakened for us to explore the biblical solution.

Illustrations to Apply

Illustrations that apply usually have the most value in terms of impact or feeling. Granted, you need to choose illustrations according to purpose. There's no use applying something if people need explanation. If they lack understanding, or don't believe something is true, there's no use trying to apply it for them. But far too many preachers seek explanation when they really need to aim for application. I think this is especially true of expository preachers because of the natural bent of exposition toward explanation. Moreover, illustrations that apply also often explain or validate. What makes an illustration applicational is that it relates truth to concrete experience. Or, as we discussed in chapter 8, it *visualizes* for people what the application looks like in their lives or the lives of others. The following hierarchy of illustrations correlates the purposes of illustrations with the connection to the audience. The hierarchy is based on the communication theory known as "identification," formulated by Kenneth Burke.[4]

High Audience Connection ⟷ Low Audience Connection

Application

Validation

Explanation

From the experience of both the speaker and listener

From listener's experience

From speaker's experience

From the experience of people we know

A true story about an unknown person's experience

"Somebody told me about . . ."

"I heard a story . . ."

"Suppose . . ."

Figure 9.2
Illustration Hierarchy

In figure 9.2 it's not difficult to see the connection between the middle box and the boxes on the left. Higher audience connection is achieved when the illustration comes from the experience of both the speaker and listeners than when the illustration is just dreamed up or involves someone whom neither speaker nor listener has ever met. But more importantly, illustrations that create high audience connection are more likely to fulfill the purpose of application or validation. When I tell my listeners that I've experienced this myself, or I say to them, "You know what it's like to experience something," there's a much higher possibility that the listeners' experience, or my experience, will validate the subject and will lead toward the listeners' practice or application of the subject. Contrast the following illustrations.

Illustration #1: One Sunday my nine-year-old daughter and I were sitting in church. Several times she had tapped me on the shoulder to ask a question during the portion of the service where we were singing and enjoying the music, trying to worship the Lord. And frankly, I had tired of all the interruptions. I was sitting there trying to worship God. Now somehow she knew better than to interrupt me during the sermon, not that it is any more important than any other part of the worship, but for some reason the interruptions stopped when the sermon started. In response to the sermon we sang a wonderful song of praise to God, giving Him glory. I was enjoying the music and worshiping the Lord from my heart with my voice when once again my daughter tapped me on the shoulder and asked me a question. In utter frustration and anger I put my arm around her, pulled her over close so that I could whisper in her ear, put my hand up so nobody would hear me, and said, "Katie, I'm trying to worship God. Shut up!" Now, we've told our kids several times that *shut up* is a bad word, it's just not something that we say, and it's not acceptable in our house or to anybody else, so both she and I were utterly shocked. And, of course, you know the second that I said that to her, and felt about half an inch high, I thought of these words that we'd been studying from James' letter: "With the tongue we praise our Lord and Father and with it we curse men who have been made in God's likeness. Out of the same mouth come praise and cursing. My brothers, this should not be."

Illustration #2: Suppose a parent with young children is sitting in church one Sunday morning, trying to worship the Lord and participate in the service, and like little children sometimes do, a son or daughter is just repeatedly seeking attention to the point of pestering that parent. And the parent finally gets so frustrated that he turns to the little child and says, "I'm trying to worship God here in this church. Now, shut up!"

Without question, the illustration from my own experience (which I shamefully confess is true) has more impact and a greater potential for both validation and application than the illustration that I might "suppose." A much better way of stating the second version of that illustration would be to begin with the words, "Some of you are young parents. Let's suppose that you are sitting in church one Sunday and you finally become so frustrated with all those little taps on your shoulder that you're tempted to turn to your child and say, . . ." That would at least give you the value of talking directly to listeners and potentially speaking to the listeners' experience, or from the listeners' experience, which is probably even more valuable than speaking from your own experience. So the illustration hierarchy is a tool that can guide your selection and creation of illustrations. First you choose illustrations according to purpose, and then you ask yourself, "If I'm trying to explain, validate, or apply, how can I do that with the greatest amount of audience connection?"

Guidelines for Using Illustrations

Following are some guidelines that I have found helpful for using illustrations. Additionally, these guidelines have received positive feedback from students with whom I have shared them.

Be sure that the illustration illustrates. As was discussed earlier in this chapter, an illustration that doesn't shed light upon something is just an isolated story, statistic, or example. The illustration must connect to the subject in order to shed light on the subject (in order to explain, validate, or apply). A story told for the sake of telling it may be entertaining or humorous, but it is not illustrative. This raises the issue of whether sermons should include stories simply for the sake of telling the story. Too many times I've heard the preacher begin, "This doesn't have anything to do with what I'm going to say this morning, but I heard this story this week and just have to share it with you." To be frank, I think that is a waste of our time in the context of worship and does not give respect to the purpose and power of preaching as an exposition of God's Word and a hearing from God's Spirit.

Illustrations must be easily understood. Like a good joke, too much explanation indicates a lack of clarity or a lack of illustration. When you tell a joke, if you have to stop and say, "Well you see the reason this is funny . . . ," then it's not a very good joke. Likewise, an illustration that requires an explanation of the illustration doesn't illustrate anything. Some explanation of the precise relationship, however, may be valuable. People have a tendency, however, to remember the illustration better than the point. So sometimes it's valuable to practice the pattern: explain, illustrate, and explain again. In other words, drive home the point you're making after stating the illustration. As mentioned above, Pastor Hybels "debriefed" the illustration so that we couldn't miss the point. This "debriefing" is not exactly succinct, but nonetheless necessary for most illustrations.

Illustrations need to be credible. Make sure that you get the facts correct. Was it 1970 or was it 1971? And who said it? Was it Richard Nixon or was it a member of his cabinet? Stories need to be believable and realistic, unless you use the absurd for the purpose of humor and laugh at it yourself. Credibility, in addition, requires giving proper credit for the illustration. The basic rule of thumb is that if another speaker (or writer) used a story to illustrate a point, don't assume credit for its illustrative power. It's easy to give credit quickly where credit is due. For example, "In his best-selling book *Dropping Your Guard* Chuck Swindoll explained it this way . . ." Even if someone did not use the material as an illustration, as you want to use it, it's still proper to cite the source if you know it. For example, "A recent *USA Today* poll indicates that . . ."

Personal illustrations help your audience identify, but the illustration should be modest, true, and discreet. Moreover, it's wise to follow the advice of Howard Hendricks, which he gave to me in my very first semester of seminary: "People will learn more from your struggles than your victories." In my years of preaching experience, I've found that he is absolutely right.

Illustrations should not only be accurate, but also appropriate. Some illustrations are appropriate for one audience but not for another, or on one occasion but not on another. In his preaching primer *Biblical Preaching*, Haddon Robinson gives an example of an illustration that may be accurate but certainly is not appropriate. Dr. Robinson writes, "One preacher trying to stress the omnipresence of God declared, 'God is even in the trash can.'"[5]

Tell an illustration instead of reading it. If the illustration is full of details, statistics, and such minutia that you absolutely must read it in order for it to be accurate, then read it, but read it well and read as little as possible. Be careful not to destroy a good illustration by not telling it well. For some excellent direction on how to tell stories well, I again commend the book *Telling Stories to Touch the Heart* by Reg Grant and John Reed.[6]

Do not use an illustration that has more impact than the big idea of the sermon. If the illustration captures the big idea vividly, then use it. Use it well. But if listeners walk away remembering the illustration and forgetting the point, the illustration may take light away from rather than shed light upon the sermon. You can keep the illustration brief to ensure that it doesn't overpower the sermon. But there's a thin line between the illustration that puts the sermon into overdrive and the illustration that overshadows.

Never twist the text to use an illustration. This guideline is perhaps the most important of all. As preachers, we need to develop an ear for the illustrative story, a good example, a powerful tale, and sometimes we hear something that is so good we think to ourselves, "That'll preach!" or "Where can I find a text to use that illustration?" Such thoughts may lead us to dangerously compromise biblical authority.

The power of the sermon is never in the illustration. The power of the sermon is in the Word of God.

Illustrations in sermon introductions should introduce the subject, raise a question that the sermon will answer, touch a need, or accomplish other goals of an introduction (see chap. 3). This is not the time to tell a story—no matter how humorous or how biblical it may be—simply for the sake of telling it. If it doesn't introduce this sermon, then the story doesn't shed light upon it. It doesn't explain, validate, or apply biblical truth.

Illustrations in sermon conclusions should drive home the sermon's big idea, synthesizing the whole sermon. The sermon's conclusion is not a place to bring up new thoughts or new material, it's the place to tie a ribbon around the entire message. The illustration that validates or applies the entire message conveys that sense of unity and force.

Don't illustrate the unknown with the unknown. In this day of increasing biblical illiteracy, a common mistake is to use an unknown Bible passage to illustrate an unknown Bible passage. In many of our North American churches, we can no longer refer to Bible characters or particular events from the Bible without at least a sentence or two of explanation.

Listeners usually perceive contemporary illustrations as more relevant than historical illustrations. As discussed in the introduction of this book, the words *relevant* and *contemporary* are not synonymous. We do need to learn from those who have gone before us, but, as indicated in the Illustration Hierarchy (figure 9.2), relevance has primarily to do with connection to the audience. And most of us more easily identify with what happens in our own context, in our own world, this week, than we do to something that happened to George Washington during the Revolutionary War.

Personal illustrations have much greater potential to apply and convince than "a story I heard" (see Illustration Hierarchy, figure 9.2). Likewise, illustrations about someone you know—used only with his or her permission—have greater potential to apply and convince than an illustration "about someone." Not only should you obtain the permission but also inform the audience that you have received permission. This takes any pressure off of that person, and it also lets people know that they can confide in you and not fear they'll show up in next Sunday's sermon. A simple one-sentence statement can let people know that you've received permission to share an illustration about someone you know. For example:

> Nancy Jones gave me permission to share a funny thing that happened to her this week at work. . . .

Before I leave the subject of personal illustrations, let me mention three important rules to follow. (I'm indebted to Haddon Robinson for these.[7]) (1) Personal illustrations must be true. I contacted a friend to get a few details about an illustration that he told from his experience. He replied, "Oh, that doesn't matter. I just made up a name to fit an anecdote I heard somewhere." He had, however, represented the story as factual and as having happened to him. He's still my friend, but his credibility dropped a bit. (2) Personal illustrations must be modest. If my personal stories always present me as the righteous hero, I'm probably violating the first rule. (3) Personal illustrations should be told without apology. If we apologize, we draw attention to something other than the illustration. If the illustration is true and accomplishes its intended purpose, no apology is necessary.

Almost any illustration is better than an illustration that comes from an illustration book. Many of my preaching colleagues will disagree with me on this guideline. And I will be the first to admit that there are rare exceptions. (Moreover, when you find that "just perfect" illustration in an illustration book, that single illustration is well worth the price of the book.) Most illustrations from illustration books (or data bases), however, are too well-known and come across as canned stories.

Again, I return to the Illustration Hierarchy and suggest that you take illustrations from the *shared* experience of both you and the listeners, or from the listeners' experience, or from your own experience, or at least from the experience of people that we know, people with real names, people that we can refer to by name, with permission, rather than the canned story. On occasion, the canned story does humorously illustrate something or raise the subject in the sermon's introduction sufficiently, but often a canned story is just that, a canned story. And it falls short of the objective of explanation, validation, or application.

Conclusion

This chapter discussed the value of using illustrations in sermons according to purpose, and provided guidelines for effective use of illustrations. One chapter for such an important topic, however, cannot suffice and so I commend to you Bryan Chapell's book *Using Illustrations to Preach with Power*. In his book he gives additional guidelines and much more of the rationale for these guidelines than I can possibly supply in one chapter.[8]

YOU TRY IT!

You may want to look at your last five sermon manuscripts to evaluate your illustrations according to the instructions in this chapter. If you want to be a little more creative and you're brave enough, give the following exercises a try.

1. *Explain* the game of baseball to a four-year-old.
2. *Convince* a four-year-old that he or she will like the game of baseball.
3. *Show* a four-year-old *how* to catch a ground ball.
4. *Listen* to a sermon by a preacher whom you respect. Evaluate his illustrations. Did they serve their purpose? How might you have illustrated the same points?

10

Be Clear!

The *general objective* in this chapter is to understand both the value of speaking clearly in preaching and the means to do so, allowing listeners to share the preacher's intended meaning.

The *specific objectives* in this chapter are

1. to obtain useful guidelines for speaking that will lead to clarity and thus foster communication (or shared meaning) between preacher and listeners;
2. to consider examples of clear speech.

One of my homiletics professors taught me the following: "If you'll just be clear, people will rise up and call you 'blessed.'" As I sat in his class, I thought, *Right! You can communicate utter heresy with clarity and people will like it!* Now that I have preached several years, however, and evaluated many students' sermons, this professor's counsel has more credibility.

One of the most simple, yet profound, definitions of communication is "shared meaning between a sender and a receiver." Thus, the sermon can have wonderful exegetical work, excellent illustrations, a relevant introduction, and appropriate applications, and the speaker can possess charisma, but if the sermon is not clear, the listeners will not share the preacher's intended meaning. Nobody will get the point. This is true not only for the sermon's thesis or big idea, but also for each move of the outline, every illustration, and the entire sermon.

It stands to reason, then, as we craft the sermon's manuscript, we must choose our words very carefully with the listeners in view. And choosing words brings us to an initial observation about words for preaching: *Words for hearing are different than words for reading.* We must write sermon manuscripts—choose our words—for the *ear* rather than the eye. The list below summarizes the differences between words for the ear and words for the eye. The list is not exhaustive, but it presents the primary distinctions in regard to clarity.

Words for Hearing Versus Words for Reading

1. When you speak, listeners cannot see chapter divisions, paragraph indentations, or subheadings.
2. When you sit down, it's over; there's no second chance.
3. Speakers must give special attention to style and delivery because the message is not as clear to the listener as it is to the speaker.
4. A listener sits at the mercy of the speaker, and a speaker, unlike a writer, must make himself understood instantly.
5. Your sermon preparation will include writing, but when composing a sermon you must choose words to be heard rather than read.

The Nature of Oral Communication

Much of what is significant about communicating clearly relates to matters of orality, or what some communication theorists refer to as "aural" communication.[1] Arthurs and Gurevich explain:

> Specifically, preachers must dwell on ideas long enough to ensure that they lodge in listener understanding. But oral communication occurs in time, not in space like the words on the

page you are now reading. As Arnold states, "Oral rhetoric is time-bound, occasion-bound, and bound to a particular human relationship previsioned, instigated, and sustained within a particular set of circumstances that pass into history as utterance ends." Once words are *spoken*, they are gone, swept away in the stream of time. Lost elements can never be regained. Experienced communicators know that audiences simply do not "get it" the first time around. Concepts must be repeated and big ideas restated if listeners are to comprehend and feel their force. Oral communicators tend to discuss ideas at their own rate, not the listener's rate. Effective oral communicators remember that the audience probably has not spent nearly as much time thinking, reading, and praying through a given issue as they have.[2]

Following are some guidelines to help speakers preach with clarity.

Guidelines for Preaching with Clarity

Observe that clarity begins in the mind. To speak clearly, we must be clear in our thinking. Clear sermons grow out of a clear sense of the big idea or homiletical proposition. In other words, communication originates in the mind, not in the mouth. Too many sermons practice the unfortunate shooting strategy of "ready, fire, aim!" To ensure clarity, a preacher must ask two essential questions: (1) What is the point I want to make? (2) What do these listeners need to hear in order to get that point?

Sermons need to be clear in expression. Oral clarity typically increases as sentence length decreases. The aim is to use short, simple sentences without getting choppy. This is a place in which the value of writing a sermon manuscript increases. Some "rules of thumb" bring clarity to expression. Never write a sentence without knowing exactly what you want to emphasize in that sentence. Never include a sentence in the sermon manuscript that doesn't need to be there. Because you're writing for the ear instead of the eye you will repeat and restate some things. Redundancy in oral communication is much more acceptable, indeed necessary, than in written communication. Never say in a compound sentence what you can say in a simple sentence or even two simple sentences. Here is a brief example.

Fair: While there are some reasons not to work out the day before a game, I believe in it because it gets the players focused on the game, comfortable with the arena, and loose physically.

Better: Some people don't like to work out the day before. I think it helps us focus and get comfortable and loose.

Another rule of thumb for clear expression is that compound sentences, like the use of the passive voice, have the disadvantage of begging for words and thus slowing the pace of the sermon. The last rule of thumb for clear expression is that in addition to simple sentences, simple words also contribute to clear expression.[3] For example:

Young advertiser of new soap product:
"The alkaline element and fats in this product are blended in such a way as to secure the highest quality of saponification along with a specific gravity that keeps it on top of the water, relieving the bather of the trouble and annoyance of fishing around for it at the bottom of the tub during his ablution."

More experienced advertiser:
"It floats."

Transitions are important. If you ask me what is the one most important guideline for clarity, I would say, "Use clear transitions between the main moves of your sermon." Transitions come in various forms: rhetorical questions, numbering, review and preview, sign-posting, and so on.[4] My favorite kind of transition—and one of the strongest forms, especially for sermons developed inductively—is the review/preview transition, which was discussed in chapter 5. So let me simply comment about numbering and the use of rhetorical questions.

Numbering can serve as flags and, therefore, transitions. For example:

First, we see that we are secure in God even when we face overwhelming odds. Second, we are secure in God, even when God's timing seems different than our timing. And there is a third awkward situation in which we are to be assured of our security.

It's important, however, to be careful with numbers. If the preacher starts numbering, at least two rules of thumb are important to ensure clarity. (1) Always have as many elements as you promise. It's very disheartening to the listener when the preacher promises four principles for holy living and then covers only three principles. (2) Never get into more than one numbering scheme at a time and use parallel key words. If the preacher says "first" and "second," only "third" (not "number three") will connect the list. A great hindrance to clarity is to start down one list of numbers and then begin a sublist within one of the numbers. I'm doing that right now as I give you two rules of thumb for our third guideline, using numbers, but it's much easier to follow this on the written page than when listening.

Another approach to transitioning is rhetorical questions. For example:

Is that all that God requires of you and me?

You're probably thinking to yourself, "Is it really that easy?"

If God loves us with an everlasting love, can we live anyway that we please?

Rhetorical questions help people to think what we want them to think as we move through the sermon and rebuild tension. Or sometimes we may combine the review/preview transition with a rhetorical question. Consider the following example:

God tells us that His blessing follows our obedience. God tells us that He delights in our obedience. But what happens when we disobey God?

Numbering also may serve as a transition. For example:

There's a third reason that we should be holy in an unholy world.

Develop main moves, or points, deductively. Even if the overall development of the sermon is inductive, main moves are much clearer when developed deductively. The following illustrates deductive development.

   I. Point

     A. Support for I

     B. Support for I

       1. Support for B

       2. Support for B

The next example contrasts the same move of a sermon, developed first inductively and then deductively.

Inductive: David's trust in the Lord teaches us well. But David must not have thought that God was coming through fast enough. In verse 7, the mood changes dramatically. It's as if David said "NOW!!!" We can trust God even when our need is urgent. Look again at verses 7–10. David anxiously pleaded for God's mercy; that is, "Hear me! Lord, I'm calling. I'm in great need." David pleaded with God on the basis of his trust in God. David sought God with a pure motive. The phrase *seek His face* is used throughout the Old Testament as an indication of one who has a pure heart before God. You cannot fool God, so there is no use even trying to seek His face deceptively. So, David's prayer is a righteous prayer. And he has a plea. "Do not hide your face," he says to the Lord, "do not refuse to help." As David indicates in verse 10, he knew that God would not forsake him. David gives the hypothetical illustration that even if his father and mother were to forsake him, he knew that God would not forsake him. David's example shows us that we must seek God even when danger is imminent. As David indicates in verses 11–12, he asked God to show him the way to go because his enemies were lying in wait for him. David asked God to deliver him from his enemies who had sworn to destroy him. Thus, David, though affirming his confidence in God, also becomes moderately panicked. When he reflects upon God's ability to deliver him from his enemies, however, he declares, "We remain secure in God even when God's timing differs from our timing." That's our second principle: We remain secure in God even when God's timing differs from our timing.

Deductive: Our second principle is that "We remain secure in God even when God's timing differs from our timing." It's as if David said "NOW!!!" We can trust God even when our need is urgent. Look again at verses 7–10. David anxiously pleaded for God's mercy; that is, "Hear me! Lord, I'm calling. I'm in great need." David pleaded with God on the basis of his trust in God. David sought God with a pure motive. The phrase *seek His face* is used throughout the Old Testament as an indication of one who has a pure heart before God. You cannot fool God; so there is no use even trying to seek His face deceptively. So, David's prayer is a righteous prayer. And he has a plea. "Do not hide your face," he says to the Lord, "do not refuse to help." As David indicates in verse 10, he knew that God would not forsake him. David gives the hypothetical illustration that even if his father and mother were to forsake him, he knew that God would not forsake him. David's example shows us that we must seek God even when danger is imminent. As David indicates in verses 11–12, he asked God to show him the way to go because his enemies were lying in wait for him. David asked God to deliver him from his enemies who had sworn to destroy him. Thus, David, though affirming his confidence in God, also becomes moderately panicked. When he reflects upon God's ability to deliver him from his enemies, however, he declares, "We remain secure in God even when God's timing differs from our timing."

In the above example, the evidence is the same in both the inductive and the deductive development. But in the deductive development, listeners do not have to wonder what all these pieces have to do with one another. The audience knows the principle that's being supported. In the inductive development, listeners do not know the principle up front. The inductive development may provide the element of surprise or "Aha!" But surprise is not usually conducive to clarity. Such an "Aha" element should be reserved for the macro structure of the whole sermon rather than used in each major point. Then the climactic advantage of inductive development allows an anticipation of the big idea throughout the entire sermon.

Develop main points in complete sentences. Phrases or fragments may be memorable but they do not give a complete thought and thus do not require the preacher or the listeners to think with precision. Consider the difference in the following example:

NOT: First, fear.

BUT: Our first response to God's holiness should be to fear Him.

Employing key words, use parallel construction at parallel levels of your outline, especially in the main points of your outline. These key words become flags, or markers, for the listener. If in Roman numeral I, you say, "The first reason to be holy in an unholy world," and in Roman numeral II, you say, "The second cause for holiness in an unholy world," it is not as clear as when both sentences give either reasons or causes. The parallel wording tells the listener that you've moved from the first reason to the second reason. This, coupled with the review/preview transitions, helps listeners move through the development of the sermon with the same clarity that you, as the preacher, have in your mind.

Two essential elements of clarity are restatement and repetition. Restatement is saying the same thing in different words. *Restatement* gives the listener the same information but in a different way. *Repetition* says the same thing using the same words. Always repeat the sermon's big idea, or homiletical proposition, and repeat and restate the main moves or points of your sermon outline. Try restating the following example: "When it seems like God isn't up to anything, be assured He's up to something." Now, *restate* that sentence in your own words.

Several factors of nonverbal communication relate to clarity. First, it's important that we use gestures purposefully. I observe the occasional preacher who has a prop engine for an arm—his hand moves through the whole sermon like a propeller. But there's no value in that gesture. In fact, it's distracting. So, use gestures purposefully, to describe something, to condense, or to emphasize a point. It's important to recall that you have only so much energy for the delivery of a sermon; calculate how you will most effectively use that energy. Moreover, be sure that the gesture matches your words. If you choose the word "huge," but hold your hands are only shoulder-width apart, the gesture distracts.

A second aspect of nonverbal communication that can increase clarity is the use of physical movement to establish your main points. Like many things in preaching, if you do this in every message, it will become so predictable that its value will decrease. But one of the ways that you can use physical movement to establish your main points is to start on the right side of the platform for point #1, and when you move to point #2, come to the center of the platform; and point #3 is reserved for the left side of the platform (left being when you face the audience). That way, in the *audience's* eyes you are moving from left to right. If in the conclusion of the message you go back to review those points, even briefly, you can move across the platform to visually remind people of the points in the sermon. Be careful not to launch into a dance in the midst of your sermon, for too much movement can be distracting. Or if you mix up the points and confuse a place on the platform with a point in the message, the nonverbal cue can be very distracting. But many listeners increase their comprehension by the cues given through the use of physical movement.

One last guideline relating to clarity, *When you're finished, conclude.* Sit down. Get out of there. Don't just stop. Don't just trail off like the old record albums used to do. Conclude. A good sermon conclusion purposes to (1) summarize the argument of the sermon, (2) drive home the big idea, and (3) call for the proper response to the message by preparing people to respond with suggested applications. (As mentioned in chap. 4, do not save all the application for the sermon's conclusion; the conclusion must, however, pave the road for the proper response in some specific ways.) Don't merely quit, even if your time is up. Conclude. Wrap it up.

Conclusion

This chapter has offered several guidelines for communicating a sermon with clarity, and yet I would be the first to admit that good, clear oral communication cannot be learned like a mathematical formula. It takes practice. It requires work—just plain hard work. So if you preach regularly, try to incorporate at least two of these guidelines in your next sermon. Then, in the next sermon add two more, and in the following sermon add two more. Eventually, the hard work will lead to good habits. And like my homiletics professor told me, "When you're clear, people will rise up and call you 'blessed.'"

YOU TRY IT!

1. Listen to radio advertising. Observe how these advertisers paint a picture or even create a drama using only words, with no television screen (and in a very short time span). Try to restate the radio advertisement in your own words.

2. Develop a paragraph to be *spoken,* not read, that describes the house in which you grew up. Use simple sentences, simple words, transitions, and repetition. Use descriptive words. Give enough detail to help listeners see what you're saying, but not so much that you lose their interest. Then, test your paragraph on a two-year-old.

3. Analyze a recent sermon manuscript, reading for transitions, repetition, and restatement. Edit the manuscript to improve its clarity. Ask a colleague, spouse, or friend to evaluate both manuscripts for clarity of the message.

Afterword

The most relevant message you can give is to stress the importance of having an intimate relationship with Jesus. That's why each semester I begin my preaching classes by asking the students to stand up, push their chairs aside, and join me in a circle on our knees. I then deliver, probably by rote memory, a "lecturette" in which I say,

> This is where relevant, biblical preaching begins, continues, and ends; from the specifics of and making exegetical decisions or 'I need an illustration,'" all the way through to praying that my heart will be right before God as I preach and that people will come prepared to hear and do the Word of God. There is absolutely no substitute for prayer and the power of the Holy Spirit in preaching.

My greatest fear with a book on communication strategies is that we may be tempted to substitute fluff for stuff. Just as there is no substitute for the power of the Holy Spirit in our preaching, there is no substitute for the power of the Word of God.[1] The message is God's Word. Without it, we have no authority. More importantly, we have nothing to say. Without God's Word, we cannot declare, "Thus says the Lord." Hence, there is no substitute for careful exegesis and theological thinking that drives our message preparation.

Likewise, I believe that God's Spirit is just as involved in the preparation of our messages as in our actual delivery. That's why I believe that good preaching begins, continues, and ends on our knees. Many times in my years of pastoral ministry I've hit a roadblock when trying to think of an illustration or perhaps how best to explain something from the text, and I've prayed. Usually within the day, the illustration or the proper way to explain something would come. I'd run it by my wife, as I do the entire sermon manuscript, and her response would be, "Oh yes, that's clear; that's very good!" There's no way for me to explain how I burst through the roadblock, apart from answered prayer.

I do not mean to suggest that our primary reason to pray in our sermonic work is utilitarian. Far more importantly, we need to pray for application of the biblical truth in our own lives before we preach it to others. While the biblical text may not give shape to the sermon, it must give shape to the preacher. Hence, we need to pray for humble hearts, righteous lives, and close fellowship with God. Trying to proclaim God's Word well without an intense love for Jesus is like trying to make an omelette without eggs.

I don't mean to spread a blanket disclaimer over this entire book, as I've seen the strategies talked about in this book work well in several pulpits. But I do want to be sure that two essential elements are understood. First, this book assumes that you understand the biblical message and have the content of God's Word to say in the sermon. Then and only then can you involve these strategies. Second, preaching is a transformative, spiritual exercise that absolutely depends on the power of the Holy Spirit, and no communication strategy can substitute for that dependence or that power.

I give thanks that some of our seminary students have caught what I'm trying to say in this Afterword. As I walked into the office one morning, I glanced at the Pastoral Ministries Department bulletin board, to discover this posting:

> We, the students of homiletics at Dallas Theological Seminary, commit to trust in God's powerful presence in our preaching. We will strive to recognize that bold and effective

preaching is a supernatural enterprise requiring our total dependence upon our Lord's supernatural enabling, resources, and authority. We pledge to pursue God's reassuring power and presence prayerfully with Spirit-filled diligence throughout every step of the privileged exposition of His Word.

A few students and faculty had signed the declaration. It was printed on a large paper with plenty of room for additional signatures. I signed gladly. I hope you will sign, too.

When I say that preaching is transformative, I'm referring to the role that preaching plays in the sanctification process that should be experienced by every believer. Paul told us in Romans 12 that we are transformed by the renewing of our minds, and preaching is one of the essential ways that God transforms our minds with His Word. So preaching is more than informative or motivational; it is transformative. Preaching is a spiritual exercise that requires a spiritual dependence of the preacher and the listener on the Spirit and Word of God. Nothing could be more relevant in our preaching than the message our lives demonstrate through an intimate love for Jesus Christ.

For we do not preach ourselves, but Jesus Christ as Lord, and ourselves as your servants for Jesus' sake.
—2 Corinthians 4:5

Preach the Word!

Notes

Introduction

1. Calvin Miller, *Marketplace Preaching: How to Return the Sermon to Where It Belongs* (Grand Rapids: Baker, 1995); Robert G. Duffett, *A Relevant Word: Communicating the Gospel to Seekers* (Valley Forge, Pa.: Judson, 1995).

2. Richard C. Halverson, *Relevance: The Role of Christianity in the Twentieth Century* (Waco, Tex.: Word, 1968).

3. Mark Galli and Craig Brian Larson, *Preaching That Connects: Using the Techniques of Journalists to Add Impact to Your Sermons* (Grand Rapids: Zondervan, 1994); and Michael Duduit, ed., *Communicate with Power* (Grand Rapids: Baker, 1996).

4. David W. Henderson, *Culture Shift* (Grand Rapids: Baker, 1998). As Scott Gibson comments on the cover, "Henderson has captured well the burgeoning generation of men and women who desperately need to hear about the Savior." *Culture Shift* is thought provoking. Henderson offers little practical directions or strategies for speaking to a shifting culture, but the book is excellent for considering the role of culture in preaching or a theology of culture.

5. Calvin Miller, *The Empowered Communicator: Seven Keys to Unlocking an Audience* (Nashville: Broadman and Holman, 1994), 3.

6. For the theoretical grounding to this definition of "communication relevance," see R. Keith Willhite, "Audience Relevance and Rhetorical Argumentation in Expository Preaching: A Historical-Critical Comparative Analysis of Selected Sermons of John F. MacArthur Jr.

and Charles R. Swindoll, 1970–1990" (Ph.D. diss., Purdue University, 1990).

7. These categories—sender, channel, message, and receiver, now common in speech communication literature—were developed in David K. Berlo, *The Process of Communication: An Introduction to Theory and Practice* (New York: Holt, Rinehart, and Winston, 1960).

8. John Piper, *The Supremacy of God in Preaching* (Grand Rapids: Baker, 1990), 17–26.

9. The double vowel indicates the divine Author (A) and the human author (a).

10. I follow Haddon W. Robinson's definition of expository preaching, found in his book, *Biblical Preaching: The Development and Delivery of Expository Messages* (Grand Rapids: Baker, 1980), 20. This is still my primer of choice. Hence, I refer to Robinson's approach to expository preaching several times in this book. In no particular order, other fine primers include Sidney Greidanus, *The Modern Preacher and the Ancient Text: Interpreting and Preaching Biblical Literature* (Grand Rapids: Eerdmans, 1988); Bryan Chapell, *Christ-Centered Preaching: Redeeming the Expository Sermon* (Grand Rapids: Baker, 1994); Walter Liefeld, *New Testament Exposition* (Grand Rapids: Zondervan, 1984); Ramesh Richard, *Scripture Sculpture* (Grand Rapids: Baker, 1995).

11. Interview with John W. Reed. His comments referenced the presentation, Bill Hybels, "Authentic Ministry: Transferable Principles," audio cassette, 1989 Pastors' Conference. Bill Hybels is founder and senior pastor of Willow Creek Community Church in South Barrington, Illinois.

12. Greg Laurie, "The Measure of a Message," Preach the Word, March 2001 (www.preachtheword.org/preach.htm).

13. A very small portion of this book was published originally as an article by the same title in Denver Seminary's magazine, *Focal Point* (summer 1996): 4–5.

Chapter 1: Look from the Pew's Perspective

1. Keith Willhite, "Relevance—Who Decides?" (Workshop presented to the National Conference on Preaching, Dallas, Tex., February 1998). A tape of this and other workshops may be ordered from Preaching Resources, Inc., P.O. Box 369, Jackson, TN 38302-0369; or by calling 1-800-288-9673.

2. I am indebted to my colleague Dr. Timothy Warren for this scheme of analysis and for his careful review of the strategy presented in this chapter. Course Handout, 603 Biblical Communication, Dallas Theological Seminary, fall 1998.

3. Ray Pritchard, *Keep Believing* (Chicago: Moody Press, 1997), 13.

4. Bill Hybels, "Speaking to the Secular Mind," *Leadership*, summer 1988, 29–30. Though Pastor Hybels' comments referred to speaking to non-Christians, I believe that his observations hold true for those listening to expository messages aimed at the edification of believers.

Chapter 2: Get into a Good Argument

1. Richard E. Crable, *Argumentation as Communication: Reasoning with Receivers* (Columbus, Ohio: Charles E. Merrill, 1976), 5–16.

Chapter 3: Whet an Appetite for God's Word

1. Kenneth Burke, *Counter-Statement* (1931; reprint, Berkeley: Univ. of California Press, 1968), 31.

2. For an expansion of this idea, see Keith Willhite, "A Sneak Peak at the Point," *Preaching*, May–June 1990, 17–22.

3. Aristotle. *On Poetics 1459a, in Aristotle: Volume II, Great Books of the Western World.* Vol. 9 (Chicago: University of Chicago and Encyclopedia Britannica, 1952), 694.

4. Steve Stroope, "God with Us in Time," a sermon preached at Lake Pointe Baptist Church, Rockwall, Tex., 13 December 1998. Used by permission.

5. Warren W. Wiersbe, *Preaching and Teaching with Imagination: The Quest for Biblical Ministry* (Wheaton, Ill.: Victor, 1994), 77.

6. John Piper, *The Supremacy of God in Preaching* (Grand Rapids: Baker, 1990), 107.

7. For valuable instruction on how to read the Bible well in public, see Thomas Edward McComiskey, *Reading Scripture in Public: A Guide for Preachers and Lay Readers* (Grand Rapids: Baker, 1991).

Chapter 4: Use Applicational Wording

1. Timothy S. Warren, "A Paradigm for Preaching," *Bibliotheca Sacra* 148 (October–December 1991): 463–86.

2. John R. W. Stott, *Between Two Worlds: The Art of Preaching in the Twentieth Century* (Grand Rapids: Eerdmans, 1982); Warren, "A Paradigm for Preaching," 463–86.

3. Haddon W. Robinson, *Biblical Preaching: The Development and Delivery of Expository Messages* (Grand Rapids: Baker, 1980), 66–68.

4. I am grateful to Linda Tomczak and Janet Johnson for the drawing of this figure.

Chapter 5: Bundle a Packaged Deal

1. H. Grady Davis, *Design for Preaching* (Philadelphia: Fortress, 1958); Haddon W. Robinson, *Biblical Preaching: The Development and Delivery of Expository Messages* (Grand Rapids: Baker, 1980). See also Keith Willhite, "A Bullet Versus Buckshot: What Makes the Big Idea Work?"; Donald R. Sunukjian, "Sticking to the Plot: The Developmental Flow of the Big Idea Sermon," in *The Big Idea of Biblical Preaching: Connecting the Bible to People,* ed. Keith Willhite and Scott M. Gibson (Grand Rapids: Baker, 1998), 13–23, 111–24.

2. Duane Litfin, *Public Speaking: A Handbook for Christians,* 2d ed. (Grand Rapids: Baker, 1992), 80. Italics in original.

3. For a fundamental and helpful approach to the strategy of unifying the sermon, see Sunukjian, "Sticking to the Plot," 111–24.

4. For excellent instruction on how to develop images and stories, see Reg Grant and John Reed, *Telling Stories That Touch the Heart* (Wheaton, Ill.: Victor, 1990), 7–35. For excellent guidance and examples of image and language of imagery, see Gary Smalley and John Trent, *The Language of Love* (Colorado Springs: Focus on the Family Publishing, 1988; rev. edition, 1991); and Warren W. Wiersbe, *Preaching and Teaching with Imagination: The Quest for Biblical Ministry* (Wheaton, Ill.: Victor, 1994).

5. See Keith Willhite, "A Sneak Peak at the Point: Sermon Introductions That Aim at Application," *Preaching,* May–June 1990, 17–22.

6. For more on maintaining tension in sermons, see Ken Bickel, "The Effect of the Introduction of Tension into Deductive Sermons on Listeners' Attention and Understanding" (D.Min. diss., Denver Seminary, June 1996).

7. I am indebted to my colleague Mitch Friedman for this valuable illustration of reviewing and previewing.

8. John Piper, *The Supremacy of God in Preaching* (Grand Rapids: Baker, 1990), 17–26.

9. Sequential exposition through a single book of the Bible is an excellent form of expository preaching. It is not, however, the only form. We may preach topical expository messages, for example, by asking,

"What does the Bible say about this topic?" The latter may require the exegesis and exposition of several passages, but the messages remain expository.

10. See Paul Borden, "Is There Really One Big Idea in That Story?" in *Big Idea of Biblical Preaching*, 67–80.

Chapter 6: Unite People, Purpose, and Proposition

1. Haddon W. Robinson, *Biblical Preaching* (Grand Rapids: Baker, 1980), 79–96. Robinson's developmental questions grow out of a tradition of long-accepted rhetorical theory from Richard Whately. Specifically compare James L. Golden and Edward P. J. Corbett, *The Rhetoric of Blair, Campbell, and Whately* (New York: Holt, Rinehart and Winston, 1968), 298.

2. Compare Eugene L. Lowry, *The Homiletical Plot: The Sermon as Narrative Art Form* (Atlanta: John Knox, 1980); and Paul Borden, "Is There Really One Idea in that Story?" in *The Big Idea of Biblical Preaching*, ed. Keith Willhite and Scott M. Gibson (Grand Rapids: Baker, 1998), 67–80.

Chapter 7: Adjust the Questions

1. Donald C. Bryant, "Rhetoric: Its Functions and Its Scope," *Philosophy, Rhetoric, and Argumentation*, ed. Maurice Natanson and Henry W. Johnstone, Jr. (University Park: Pennsylvania State Univ. Press, 1965), 47. Originally published in *Quarterly Journal of Speech* 39 (1953): 401–24.

2. John Piper, *Desiring God* (Portland, Ore.: Multnomah, 1986), 41.

3. Ibid.

4. Haddon W. Robinson, *Biblical Preaching* (Grand Rapids: Baker, 1980), 115–34.

5. For example, see Michael S. Hanna and James W. Gibson, *Public Speaking for Personal Success*, 2d ed. (Dubuque, Ia.: Wm. C. Brown, 1989), 164–65.

Chapter 8: Tell 'n Show

1. Michael Hodgin, *1001 Humorous Illustrations for Public Speaking* (Grand Rapids: Zondervan, 1994), 263.

2. Reg Grant and John Reed, *Telling Stories to Touch the Heart* (Wheaton, Ill.: Victor, 1990), 35.

Chapter 9: Illustrate According to Purpose

1. I developed this ludicrous definition of something that is quite simple from several dictionary definitions.
2. Ian MacPherson, *The Art of Illustrating Sermons* (New York: Abingdon, 1964).
3. Bill Hybels, "Trying to Run On Empty" (audiotape, Willow Creek Community Church, South Barrington, Ill., October 1993).
4. Kenneth Burke, *A Rhetoric of Motives* (1950; reprint, Berkeley: Univ. of California Press, 1962), 19–46. Burke's theory of identification involves more than simply connections through similarities, but in a nutshell, Burke describes identification as follows: "A is not identical with his colleague, B. But insofar as their interests are joined, A is *identified* with B. Or A may *identify himself* with B even when their interests are not joined, if A assumes that they are, or is persuaded to believe so" (20).
5. Haddon W. Robinson, *Biblical Preaching* (Grand Rapids: Baker, 1980), 152.
6. Reg Grant and John Reed, *Telling Stories to Touch the Heart* (Wheaton, Ill.: Victor, 1990).
7. Robinson, *Biblical Preaching*, 153–54.
8. Bryan Chapell, *Using Illustrations to Preach with Power* (Grand Rapids: Zondervan, 1992).

Chapter 10: Be Clear!

1. See Walter Ong, *Faith and Contexts*, ed. Thomas J. Farrell and Paul A. Soukup (Atlanta: Scholars Press, 1992); John Miles Foley, ed., *Oral Tradition: A Festschrift for Walter J. Ong* (Columbus, Ohio: Slavica, 1987).
2. Jeffrey Arthurs and Andrew Gurevich, "Proclamation Through Conversation: Dialogue as a Form for Preaching," *Journal of the American Academy of Ministry* 5 (winter–summer 1997): 40. They cite Carroll C. Arnold, "Oral Rhetoric, Rhetoric and Literature," in *Contemporary Rhetoric: A Reader's Coursebook*, ed. Douglas Ehninger (Glenview, Ill.: Scott Foresman, 1972), 70.
3. For exceptional advice on speaking with economy, subtlety, and paced energy, see Sue Nichols, *Words on Target: For Better Christian Communication* (Atlanta: John Knox, 1963).

4. For an excellent discussion on transitions, see Duane Litfin, *Public Speaking: A Handbook for Christians*, 2d ed. (Grand Rapids: Baker, 1992), 189–94.

Afterword

1. A helpful balance is presented in Dennis F. Kinlaw, *Preaching in the Spirit* (Nappanee, Ind.: Francis Asbury Press, 1985).

About the Author

Keith Willhite serves as Department Chairman and Professor of Pastoral Ministries at Dallas Theological Seminary. Prior to joining the faculty of Dallas Seminary in 1996, he served ten years in pastoral ministry and then as Chairman of the Department of Homiletics and Director of the D.Min. Program at Denver Seminary. Dr. Willhite earned his Ph.D. in communication from Purdue University and his Th.M. from Dallas Seminary. He teaches expository preaching and research methods for ministry, and is founder of the ministry consulting group *Strategenuity*.